A Portrait of Grief and Courage

**Documented and Photographed
by Sandra Shackelford**

May Lee Lor,
Interpreter and Collaborator

Ma Lee Lor,
Translator and Transcriber

Published by
Mimi & Rupert Books
an imprint of The Teaching Press at UW-Green Bay
uwgb.edu/teaching-press

Located at The Maker Space, Room 158
2019 Technology Way
Brown County STEM Innovation Center
Green Bay, WI 54311

ISBN 979-8-9855031-4-2

Cover design by Emily Heling
Cover photograph of Mai Xiong by Sandra Shackelford
Interior design by Emily Heling
Interior photographs and artwork by Sandra Shackelford

Table of Contents

Preface by Pao Lor- *i*

Introduction - *v*

A Note About the Text- *xv*

Part I- Oral Histories and Interviews

Pa Lee- Please Give Me the Words to Speak My Grief- *2*

Thor Xiong (Thao Chang)- Interview- *7*

Thor Xiong (Thao Chang)- A Deaf Woman's Prayer- *17*

Mai Xiong- Interview- *19*

Mai Xiong- The Healer- *37*

Nyoua Thao- Life in Camp- *46*

Mee Lee- What I Have Seen is Very Bad- *48*

Thao Chong- There is Nothing That Will Compare With This Talk- *51*

Yee Vang- Night in a Pig Pen- *52*

Pa Thao- A Woman Alone- *60*

Xay Lue Yang- Life in Laos: Then and Now- *63*

Sao Soua Ly- A Life- *69*

Nor Chia Lor- I Will Tell You What I Know- *89*

Part II- Oral Histories and Folktales

Da Thao- A Story of Survival- *99*

Mai Yang- The Way of Neeb- *103*
(Healing Ceremony)

Glossary of Shamanic Terms- *113*

Folktales

Orphan and the Ghost- *114*

The Frog, the Crab, and the Muskrat- *119*

Orphan Finds a Wife- *123*

The Story of the Rainbow- *127*

Orphan and the King's Daughter- *134*

Part III- Oral Histories and Myths

Sandra Shackelford- A Journey Home- *143*

You Thoua Lor- Now the People Are Telling It- *145*

The Myth of Yeng Saki- *146*

You Thoua Lor's Ending-*171*

Sources- *173*

Acknowledgements- *174*

Biographies- *175*

A Note About the Design- *179*

Preface

Hmong Oral Storytelling Intersects Literacy

Pao Lor

Oral storytelling is a pantheon of the Hmong experience. The Hmong use it to pass on their history, identity, cultural practices and norms, wisdom, life lessons, and family lineage, illuminating the sophistication, intricacy, nuance, and complexity of the Hmong experience.

In 1975, Hmong oral storytelling took an abrupt turn when the United States (U.S.) pulled out of the Secret War in Laos, a clandestine military operation supported by the U.S. to stop the spread of communism in Southeast Asia. As allies of the U.S. during the Secret War and fearing ethnic persecution, many Hmong fled to Thailand as refugees, and then the majority eventually resettled in the U.S. The first Hmong families arrived in the U.S. in 1975, and thousands soon followed. Amid the challenges and triumphs of a new life, oral storytelling initially thrived within the seamless network of Hmong communities across the U.S. It provided cultural salvation, safety, and a sense of belonging for many Hmong. However, soon, day by day and year by year, its role, value, and relevance diminished.

Factors impacting the change included fewer opportunities for Hmong storytellers to practice their craft, new Hmong generations transitioning and adapting to the literate world, less emergent Hmong storytellers, the Hmong written language that was developed in the 1950s becoming more relevant in the Hmong communities, among others. From the 1990s and to the early 2000s, Hmong oral storytelling, in its traditional form and context, became dormant, nearing extinction. A decade ago, a rebirth of the Hmong oral storytelling experience took place. The rebirth is a seamless tie between technology such as YouTube, Facebook, and recording programs and the newly established global Hmong network. "With the sun shining on all Hmong people around the world," there was a need for Hmong to reconnect, and that need, coupling with many Hmong still relying on oral or word of mouth communications, resuscitated Hmong oral storytelling. Our ancestors, elders, and prior oral storytellers could not have imagined this new form of Hmong oral storytelling experience.

Today, Hmong oral storytellers select stories submitted by readers, record them with sound effects and pictures, and then share them via Youtube and Facebook with listeners around the world. Listeners simply need to have a smart phone and access to the Internet to take part in this new oral telling experience. They can do it while farming in remote villages throughout Southeast Asia, relaxing in a posh apartment in Paris, vacationing on a beach resort in Thailand, hiking in the Rocky Mountains in Utah, driving on Highway 101 on the Pacific Coast, enjoying a cruise in the Caribbean, hunting and fishing, and so on. Unlike prior generations, today's Hmong oral storytellers and listeners do not have to wait until the end of an exhaustive day to gather to tell, enjoy, learn from, relax, and be entertained by a variety of compelling Hmong stories on various themes from all walks of life.

The new generation of Hmong oral storytellers are eloquent, insightful, and engaging, just like prior generations. With over five decades of new Hmong experiences to draw from, they are not limited to fairy tales, folktales, myths, and legends. Their stories are more expansive and inclusive: migration, domestic abuse, lost love, life lessons, triumphs, women's empowerment, gender-equity, social justice, miseries, greed, generosity, inter-racial marriages, racial and ethnic experiences, mental health, supernatural and spiritual experiences, cultural practices, among others.

Today, Hmong oral storytelling is vibrant and relevant as it was in the past, but it has limitations. It only reaches Hmong speaking audiences. So, begs the question: can the sophistication, intricacy, nuance, and complexity of the Hmong experience be shared with a universal audience, including newer Hmong generations that are not proficient in the Hmong language, to inform and advance the human conditions? This is where the Hmong experience and Hmong oral storytelling intersect with the literate world. *A Portrait of Grief and Courage* is a window into such intersectionality.

May there be more.

Dr. Pao Lor is the Associate Dean of the School of Education at University of Wisconsin—Lacrosse. He grew up in Green Bay, Wisconsin, and is the author of *Modern Jungles: A Hmong Refugee Story of Survival* (Madison: Wisconsin Historical Society Press, 2021).

Southeast Asia

CHINA

VIETNAM

MYANMAR
(BURMA)

LAOS

Gulf of
Tonkin

● Ban Vinai
Refugee Camp

Mekong River

THAILAND

CAMBODIA

Gulf of
Thailand

South
China
Sea

0 100 kilometers

0   100 miles

Map by Amelia Janes,
Midwest Educational Graphics

Introduction

Rebecca Meacham and Olivia Meyer

"When you interview someone, you follow their history. It's not about you."

— Sandra Shackelford

The journey you are about to embark on has been decades in the making. The story of the Hmong people in Northeast Wisconsin has lived alongside, and outside, traditional historical narratives. This rich history has been overlooked for many reasons, including the fact that Hmong culture is based heavily in oral traditions. *A Portrait of Grief and Courage* is a collection of those oral stories, documented for the first time and accompanied by photographs of the storytellers in their homes in Green Bay, Wisconsin.

These stories begin in Laos, where, during the Vietnam War, Hmong people living in Laos were recruited by the CIA to fight in support of the United States in an operation known as the Secret War. When the United States withdrew from the war, the Hmong people were persecuted by the Vietnamese. They fled to refugee camps in Thailand before being admitted into the United States in the late 1970s. Wisconsin was one of the leading destinations for rehoming refugees.

A Voice from the Darkness

Settling into life in the U.S. in the 1980s and 1990s presented radical new challenges to the Hmong people. Life in Laos had entailed farming with hand tools, struggling through rice shortages, moving from village to village, hiding in the jungle from Communist soldiers, walking a mile in bare feet to get water, and catching spiders and grasshoppers to eat. Life in the U.S. entailed refrigerators, grocery stores, street names, health care systems, public transportation. Meeting basic needs could be overwhelming: How do you run the shower? How do you turn on a stove? How do you do laundry? How do you get health checkups for your family? What do you say to people when you greet them? When you go to a public place, how do you get to the bathroom? How do you ask other people for help?

To provide aid in the early 1990s, Northeast Wisconsin Technical College's High Risk Family Support Program sent individuals to visit newly settled refugees in their homes. Sandra Shackelford was one of these volunteers. Sandra was joined by translator May Lee Lor, who, along with this project's transcriber Ma Lee Lor, had been children when their families had made the harrowing journey to the United States a decade earlier. As Ma Lee recounts, "When my family came over in the 1980s, we didn't have resources because there weren't enough Hmong to help. To me, it was easy to help Hmong families in a heartbeat, because I'd had the same experience."

On one visit in January, with temperatures at 20-below zero, Sandra and May Lee encountered the woman who inspired the project that ultimately became this book. In Sandra's words:

> We pushed the door and it opened. There in the middle of the room was a scene that broke both of our hearts. A baby, wrapped in a blanket, sat tied into an infant car seat, flames shooting out of the apartment's only heat source, a grate-less gas heater.
>
> A shadow in the dark corner of the room moved. Slowly a woman walked toward us. Tears streamed down her face. She pointed toward me and spoke to May Lee in Hmong.
>
> This is what she said. "Please give me the words to speak my grief."

Sandra heard this plea as a call to action. Joined by her collaborators, she began gathering the stories of Green Bay's resettled Hmong residents and photographing their families, activities, and traditional folk and storytelling practices.

Sandra Shackelford and the Art of Compassion

As a documentarian and artist, Sandra Shackelford has long felt a responsibility to facilitate social change through her work. Her sense of mission began in high school. After a childhood spent performing as a dancer, she'd grown into a social but academically limited teenager, when a nun at her school told Sandra she "was not very bright" but had "a nice personality"— and there was a place that could use her. That place was Greenwood, Mississippi, the home of the White Citizens' Council. That summer between her junior and senior year, she taught bible school to five-year-old Black children. Sandra joined Black and

White female members of Pax Christi Secular Institute at St. Francis Center to teach Bible School and support the community. Prior to graduating from high school in 1958, her summer volunteer work in Mississippi was recognized and she was presented with a Lumen Christi award, the Catholic Extension's highest honor for community service.

By then, as Sandra puts it, "my life had changed forever."

For the next 11 years, she dedicated her life and work to Pax Christi and the Franciscan mission of "sowing love" through working for civil and human rights in the Mississippi Delta. She created a kindergarten based on the teaching methods of Maria Montessori and co-edited what became an early printed voice of the community's Black population. Titled *The Center LIGHT*, the weekly paper sought to "give people the light, and they will find their way." All around her were relentless threats and violence. Crop duster planes dropped leaflets on the city calling Pax Christi members "Communists." The Ku Klux Klan hurled a firebomb at the newspaper's office. Flames charred the office's white cement block exterior.

The unrelenting cruelty nearly broke her spirit. As she recalls, "Every day I sensed my own smallness in the face of it. Every day I felt responsible for it. And for twenty years after, I carried that responsibility with me."

Sandra returned to Green Bay in the late 1960s in despair, searching for ways to put her compassion—her sense of responsibility for the suffering of others—to work. Her artistic talents became a guiding light. She wrote articles as a journalist in the Fox Valley, earned her B.A. through University of Wisconsin-Green Bay's returning adults program, served as an instructor of life drawing and anatomy at UW-GB and St. Norbert College in De Pere, WI, and became a writing specialist at the College of the Menominee Nation.

In Green Bay, Sandra found she could use the practices of art and creative writing to help people speak their truths, relieve loneliness, and overcome trauma. She created Writing Circles and worked with people who'd experienced violence and sexism, encouraging them to find their own voices—and value in their lives. Ultimately, the art of compassion helped Sandra find value in herself.

When, in the 1990s, she connected with the NWTC's Family Support Program and May Lee Lor and Ma Lee Lor, Sandra found more than a new way to serve a marginalized community. She uncovered stories and folktales, celebrated joys, and bore witness to harrowing pain. She discovered a way, through the gathering of oral histories, to preserve the long-held silent grief of Hmong people and share their experiences with generations to come.

As Sandra puts it, "Meeting people of courage, human beings who survived unimaginable trauma—witnessing the death of friends and loved ones, the destruction of their homes and villages—documenting these experiences, will stay with me throughout my life. Their spoken stories not only taught me what courage looks like, and is, but also served as a long-needed healing balm for my own leftover depression after witnessing inhumanity in the racist South."

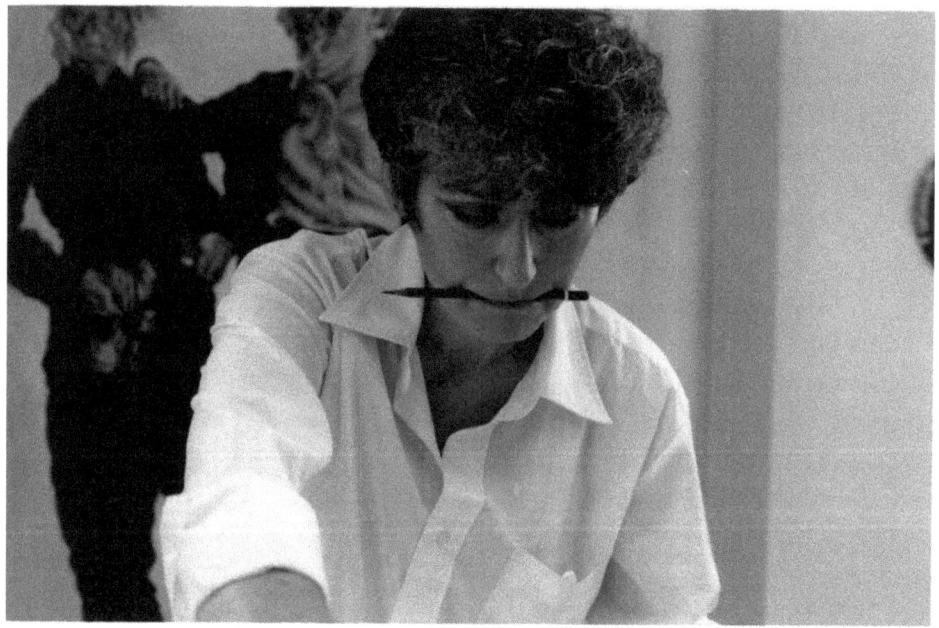

Sandra Shackelford at work in her studio in 1991.
Sandra Shackelford Collection, University of Wisconsin-Green Bay, Archives Department.

Capturing **A Portrait**

The voice from the darkness that January morning was that of Pa Lee, a 57-year-old woman grieving the loss of her family in Laos, yet grateful for the comforts she'd found in Green Bay. Several others followed. Fourteen of these voices are collected in *A Portrait of Grief and Courage*.

Their stories were gathered in two ways. In interviews, Sandra would ask questions and May Lee would translate; these exchanges are presented in interview format in this book. Alternatively, when people wished to record their stories privately, Sandy and May Lee left them the tape recorder, then delivered the recordings to May Lee for translation. These accounts are presented in this book as narratives. In the cases when a single subject was interviewed and provided separate narrative recordings, both kinds of accounts are presented in separate chapters.

These 14 voices recount personal and collective grief as well as moments of courage, judgment, and humor. From them, we learn that in Laos, some endured crippling poverty while others thrived. As Xay Lue Yang says in "Life in Laos," "We found our food easily and as often as we wished. We had nothing to worry about. When we looked for food or for work, we didn't need any kind of writing on paper. We had ideas." We read how decades of war and turmoil in Southeast Asia impacted local and clan politics. We hear how women fled persecution by North Vietnamese soldiers across the Mekong River, bribed officials with gold earrings, lost precious healing herbs to gunfire, and nursed babies amidst constant hunger. We learn how men became soldiers for the French because taxes were too steep to maintain family farms. We hear opinions of political leaders, especially General Vang Pao, an ethnic Hmong commander of the CIA-supported "Secret Army," whose evacuation from Laos after the 1975 fall of Vientiane led, ultimately, to the exodus of thousands of Hmong people to refugee camps and eventual resettlement in the United States. At the same time, we're charmed by the interactions between Sandra and her subjects, as with Mai Xiong, who claims to be 120 years old, and Yee Vang, whose husband "is not cute! I don't know why I married him!" We read tales—some silly, some disgusting— about Orphan Boy, an underdog figure in Hmong folktales who struggles to make a living outside his homeland and, through hard work, perseveres.

Once gathered, the accounts were translated and transcribed. As we state in our "Note About the Text," not everything translated easily from Hmong into English, or from oral story into print. In addition, translations were impacted by generational differences between the elderly speakers, who'd spent their lives speaking Hmong, and the translators who'd moved to the U.S. as children, learned English, and spoke Hmong less and less. Yet those generational differences fostered new connections for the translators. Xay Lue Yang, the speaker of "Life in Laos," is the father of May Lee Lor, who says she learned details about his life from his recorded words. Similarly, when Ma Lee Lor began translating and transcribing the chapter "The Way of Neeb," a narrative about Mai Yang's Shamanic practices, she turned to her father—a well-known Shaman back in Laos—for guidance, bringing them closer together: "It's one thing that made my heart kind of involved."

Sandra, too, forged deep connections with the people she interviewed. On living room couches, she was shown family photos and listened to tales stitched into story cloths. Children presented her with their illustrated versions of folktales. Men invited her to rituals, "to sit at their table while they were proving their manhood." She helped with ceremonies where she stirred a pot of blood and other liquids. Along the way, she captured many intimate moments in photographs and drawings.

Indeed, what makes this collection unique among Hmong oral histories is its presentation of voices alongside Sandra's original photographs and pencil drawings. Such images add layers of meaning and emotional depth to the speakers' testimonies. For instance, in the chapter "A Life," a narrative by Sao Soua Ly, we see Ly seated in the shadows beside a bright window. As a photographer, Sandra was drawn to the space around Ly because "it reflects the absence of what she's lost. It's a loneliness you can see." Although only a handful of photos are presented in this book, Sandra developed hundreds of images in her own darkroom—and used some prints to create large-scale pencil drawings. This process, too, was guided by her compassion. As she explains, "the wrinkles, ruffles, and folds in a drawing take me on a journey inside. They help me see the person on the inside—and to see myself." In this way, Sandra's creative process is, as she puts it, "both a caress and a dissection."

Prior to 2023, some drawings, images, and narratives were exhibited through museums and galleries around Wisconsin, including the Neville Public Museum in Green Bay, the Brown County Library, the Miller Art Museum in Sturgeon Bay, and the Hardy Gallery in Ephraim. Sandra later collaborated again with Ma Lee Lor on "Connected by a Thread," an artistic study of women's stitchwork, handwork, and embroidery. In addition, an earlier version of this manuscript— assembled in 1995 with additional narratives, photographs, and the original cassette recordings— is available in the UW-Green Bay Cofrin Library Archives, as part of the new Sandra Shackelford collection.

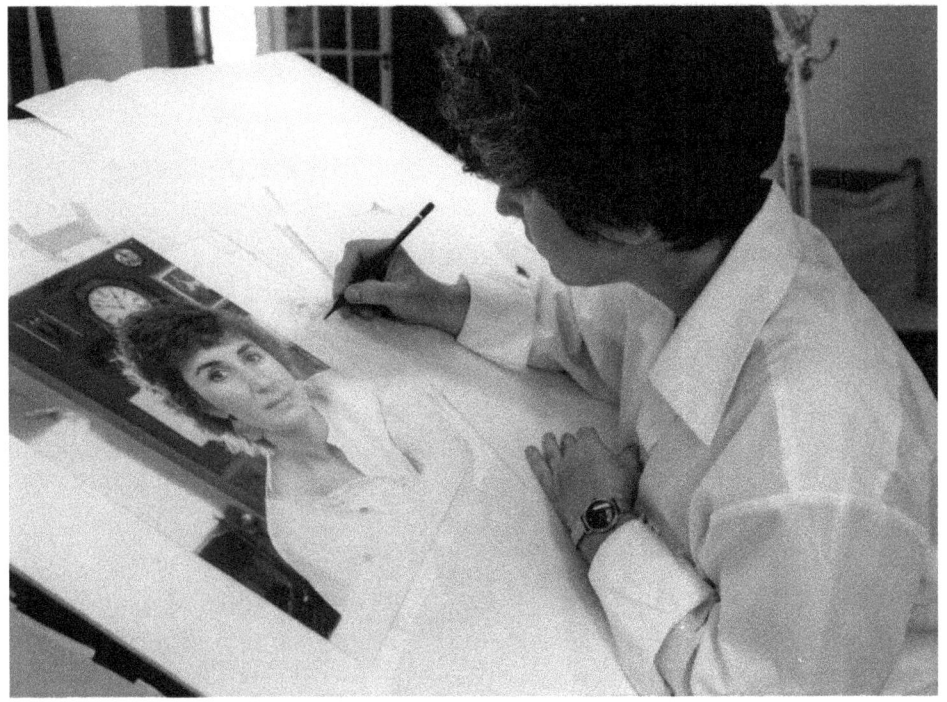

Sandra Shackelford at work in her studio in 1991.
Sandra Shackelford Collection, University of Wisconsin-Green Bay, Archives Department.

"No one is ever going to understand what others have gone through without reading."
— Ma Lee Lor

As an artist, Sandra Shackelford positions herself in each of her projects as a collaborator rather than the sole author. In this way, she captures moments of personal significance and collective history for audiences of all backgrounds. As she puts it, "It is my deepest hope that *A Portrait of Grief and Courage* will connect readers, and that in learning to respect and love one another, we will be able to find peace as individuals and as a common and shared humanity."

Sandra's collaborators also see a link to a fading past. As interpreter May Lee Lor states, "In the 1980s, when people just started to come to the U.S., there was a lot of prejudice against the Hmong people. The elders wanted to explain why we were here, and it was important for Sandy and me to collect their stories. These stories are good to have, because now they're gone." Transcriber Ma Lee Lor agrees: "We're never ever going to hear that same kind of speaking style from these elders anymore. Those times were lived by those people at that time, and many of them have all gone. But in the late 1980s, they were captured at the moment, and now we still have them. We had to put it on paper so younger generations like myself can understand and relate. No one is ever going to understand what others have gone through without reading."

As you read, you'll feel the urgency of these voices, who over and over want their stories heard, retold, and understood. Pa Lee prays "for the world to tell my grief to and to have it written down as a story for my children." Mee Lee wants "to tell you about our country and how we lived and did things and about how poor we were." At the end of his self-recording, Xay Lue Yang beseeches his listeners: "Everyone, if you listen to this, please pardon and excuse me. For those of you who are more well off, please love the people who are orphans and who are poor."

These voices implore us to listen and to understand. Doing so, as Sandra knows, is our responsibility. "There is so much prejudice in the world," she says. "If we can share stories and the lives of other people, we will become more sensitive. For readers that know nothing, you will gain some compassion. For Hmong people, you will know your stories are being heard. In an age where people don't respect each other, my gift to the world is compassion."

Dr. Rebecca Meacham is the Founder, Director, and Publisher of The Teaching Press at UW-Green Bay, and its imprints, Mimi & Rupert Books and Hard Penned Press. She is the author of three collections of prose and a professor of Writing and Applied Arts, English, and Humanities.

Olivia Meyer is the Project Manager for *A Portrait of Grief and Courage: Hmong Oral Histories and Folktales*. She also served as event coordinator for another Teaching Press title, *Wandering Toft Point: A Nature Journal*. She will graduate from UW-Green Bay in December, 2023, with a B.F.A. in Writing and Applied Arts.

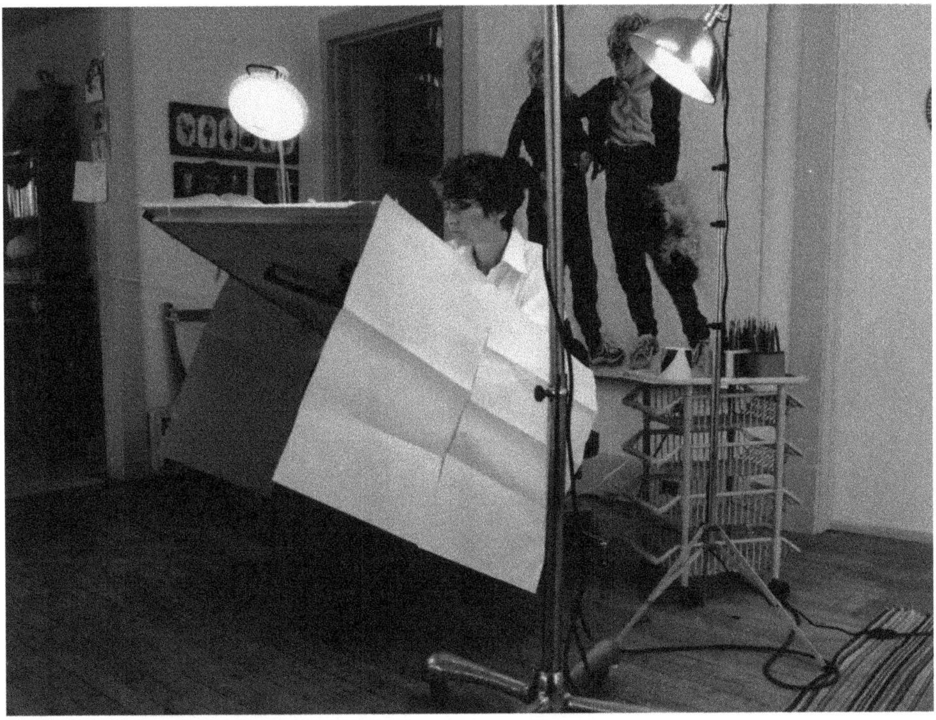

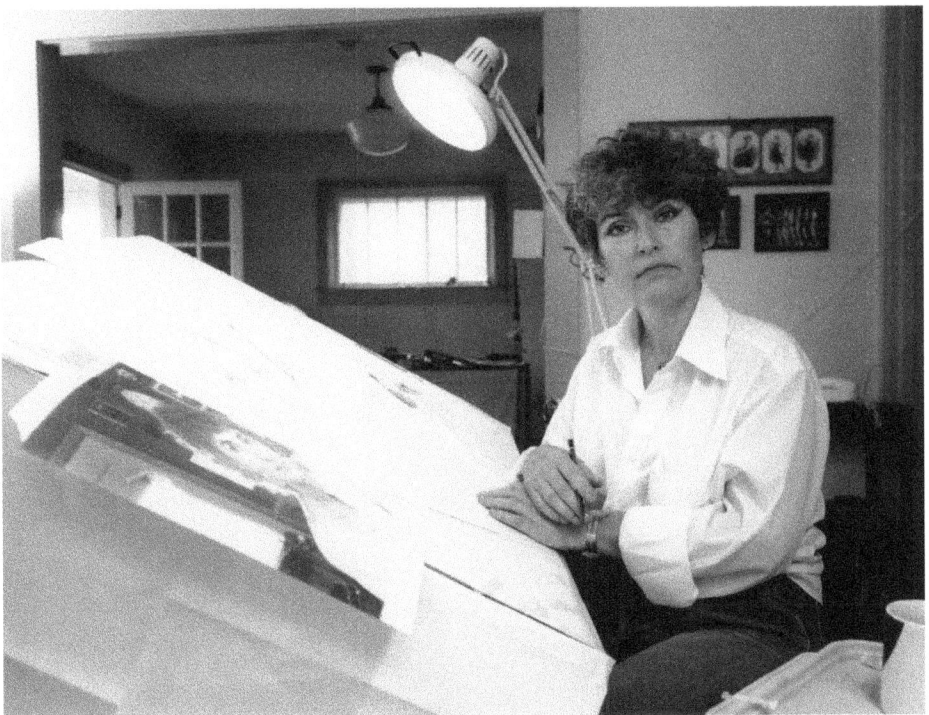

Sandra Shackelford at work in her studio in 1991.
Sandra Shackelford Collection, University of Wisconsin-Green Bay, Archives Department.

A Note About the Text

Katherine Halfman, Chief Copyeditor

A Portrait of Grief and Courage: Hmong Oral Histories and Folktales presented a multitude of distinct editorial challenges. The first challenge was time: nearly all of the work of gathering, translation, and transcription was completed in the early 1990s. As described in the "Introduction" to this book, the live interviews with Sandra Shackelford were translated from Hmong into English and interpreted by May Lee Lor; Ma Lee Lor also translated and transcribed the testimonies made privately on cassette tapes. Since making these original recordings, some of the speakers in this book have returned to Laos; others moved elsewhere, or passed away. For these reasons, when The Teaching Press acquired the collection in 2023, we were unable to ask the original speakers for clarifications or additions.

Another challenge came with identifying some of the locations and cultural practices named in this book. Because some villages and towns in these stories have been renamed or no longer exist, we sought help from Hmong speakers in our local community, who generously volunteered their time and support. Dr. Pao Lor, who wrote this book's "Preface," and who recounts his own experience as a Hmong refugee in Green Bay, WI, in *Modern Jungles: A Hmong Refugee Story of Survival*, helped our Teaching Press team properly identify and spell the names of many of the mentioned locations in Laos and Thailand. Working from the manuscript, Doua Lor, the Southeast Asian Specialist Safe Harbor of Sheboygan County Inc., assisted our team with Shamanic terms in "The Way of Neeb" chapter. Our editors also spoke with May Lee Lor and Ma Lee Lor about their translation process in the early 1990s.

Indeed, the biggest challenges in creating this book came before The Teaching Press acquired the manuscript: translating words from Hmong to English, and from an oral-based language into print. Ma Lee Lor said of the process of transcribing, "We would listen to tapes and interviews and I would write exactly what they said. What gets lost is a lot of the tonal poetic ways of talking. There's a lot of repetition because that is how the language is. They speak in run-ons with no periods—It's like comma this, comma that. Do I need to write that again? She already said that." Likewise, May Lee Lor, who helped translate the interviews as they were conducted, said, "What gets lost in the process of taking interviews and stories from an oral culture, translated into English, then transcribed into a print-based language, English has more words than in Hmong. English is backwards from Hmong—what we say in English is Hmong backwards."

Working through these challenges, we've tried to create a clean, readable text without sacrificing the original speech patterns of the speakers, who are themselves from different backgrounds, each with their own unique voice, style, and perspective. We approached editing with a light touch, making small changes for clarity while prioritizing the original voice of the interviewees and the cadence of the Hmong language. To preserve the speakers' repetitions, sentence order, sentence fragments and run-ons, and verb tenses, The Teaching Press enacted strict copyediting guidelines, most of which contradicted our team's conventional, English-based copyediting training.

Beyond the significance this book holds for the interviewees and their families, it also serves as a primary historical source, containing firsthand accounts from life in Laos, refugee camps, and the Secret War. This added another layer of difficulty to our editing process, especially when we sought to verify certain information: without access to the interviewees, we were unable to ask for more detail. Ultimately, we retained passages even when the meaning may still be unclear; this is because we would rather maintain the integrity of the interviewee's original words than potentially misconstrue their meaning.

As with most published oral histories, we corrected spelling, standardized dates and punctuation, and omitted false starts as well as filler words such as "you know." We used typography to denote the many asides and additions throughout the text, some of which were added for clarity by Ma Lee Lor, some of which were added for context by Sandra, and some of which indicate some kind of action from the interviewee, like laughter or a specific gesture. Each of these categories requires its own visual indicator, and we decided on the following:

- Parentheses denote an interviewee's actions during an interview. Example: They went to fight the war and he die. (Laughs in irony).
- Italics in parentheses indicate asides from Sandra Shackelford or May Lee Lor that establish history or background. Example: *(Here Mai Xiong contradicts herself, saying she is oldest, second oldest.)*
- Brackets indicate words added by Ma Lee Lor, Doua Lor, or our team for clarity. Example: One reason why I am able to heal is that my Da Neeb [shaman spirits] took me straight to it and was able to

get my kids, my kids here, my two kids for me.

- In sections where Ma Lee Lor was unable to decipher what was said on a cassette recording, we denoted this with "[inaudible]."

Finally, we also made the choice to change all instances of "Lao" when describing a person or group of people to "Laotian;" the difference between the two being that Lao is an ethnic group, whereas any person or thing from Laos is Laotian. While some of the people referred to may well have been Lao, we have no way to verify the identity of every person mentioned, so we made the decision to avoid potential assumptions of ethnicity. Other referenced groups, like the Viet Cong and the Hmong Vietnamese (denoting Hmong who worked alongside the Vietnamese), have been left as they were originally mentioned to maintain the voice of the interviewees.

Katherine Halfman is the Chief Copyeditor for *A Portrait of Grief and Courage: Hmong Oral Histories and Folktales*. She will graduate from UW-Green Bay in December, 2023, with a B.F.A. in Writing and Applied Arts.

Part I

Oral Histories and Interviews

The first-floor apartment was vacant. There was no heat in the building. May Lee and I climbed the stairs to the second floor. The apartment door was open a crack. We called out. No one answered. We pushed the door and it opened.

There in the middle of the room was a scene that broke both of our hearts. A baby, wrapped in a blanket, sat tied into an infant car seat, flames shooting out of the apartment's only heat source, a grate-less gas heater.

A shadow in the dark corner of the room moved. Slowly a woman walked toward us. Tears streamed down her face. She pointed toward me and spoke to May Lee in Hmong.

This is what she said:

"Please give me the words to speak my grief."

Please Give Me the Words to Speak My Grief

Pa Lee

Pa Lee looking out her window.

Sandra Shackelford Collection, University of Wisconsin-Green Bay, Archives Department.

A long time ago, I was born to my mom and dad, who were called Ga Neng Lee. They lived in Khang Kay. I was born there. Then we moved to a town called Sang Hou, where I grew up. After that comes General Vang Pao's War.

Then the Vietnamese came to Sang Hou and broke us up. We ran to Longcheng, where we lived. I got married to my husband there. After we had been married for 14 years, the Vietnamese communists came to our village, in 1975. General Vang Pao had run away to a different country—to America. He left us. We were very poor, and we all cried very much.

The communists were very bad to us. We ran after Vang Pao.

We got to a town called Hin Heup, halfway to Vientiane. The communists tried to kill us there. They shot at us for one hour and then we ran back to a town called Muang Cha. We couldn't live there because the communists were very bad to us.

My husband took my family to live in the jungle. We lived there for six years. We had nowhere to go, just in the jungle. We didn't have crops or food or salt to eat. The Vietnamese were looking for us every day. We lived in the jungle, and we were very scared. We ate only tropical roots. Just grinding it and then steaming it to make it edible like rice, for six years. They killed my husband.

My children and I were very scared. We had no food to eat and we couldn't find horseradish root to cook, and no salt. No rice to eat. We cried very much, and we were very scared of the Vietnamese finding us. I lived with my children.

My children and I lived in the jungle alone for five months. We couldn't go anywhere. We heard about some Hmong living in a town called Poua Moua Thao who were going to move to Thailand. That's why my children and I came. And at the time, my husband had already died.

My first daughter was eight years old. My second daughter, six years old. My son was four years old. And I was very poor and so depressed because my children were so small.

My children and I walked through rocks, mountains, and canyons for 20 days. Then we got to Pou Moua Chao. That town was surrounded by woods and jungles, and we were starving. We couldn't get any real food to eat, just those horseradish roots.

We were very poor. My children were very small. No one helped us and I was so poor, I just cried every day. We were very hungry, always starving. Some days you couldn't even get one root for the children to eat. Just one per day for all of us, my children and me. I had to cut it into small pieces. One piece per person. And we were very hungry. My children were very small and skinny. Even though we were so weak, somehow, we lived.

I am their mother, and I was very poor. I cried very much. At the time I had no relatives. I wanted to flee to Thailand but I couldn't go. None of my relatives were still with us, so I became very poor. But there was still one of my husband's relatives. His clan was Vang, too. He said, "You are very poor." And that is why I got married to this person, because my children were very small and there was no one to help build a house for the children. And when the sun is up, you start up a fire and let the kids sit around the fire. And you, as a mother, must go find roots for the children to eat. If it rains, they just sat under a tree. And I was so very poor. This relative of my husband, he saw us and he loved us very much. He felt sorry for us. That is why we got married. And then he helped look for food. He tried to get roots for us to eat and helped build a house for the children.

I had been married to him eight years and we were still living in the jungle, too. And the Vietnamese kept looking for us in the jungle. We couldn't make one day's crop, just eating horseradish root, wild bananas, and wild bushes.

"My mother. If we ran to Thailand and if they spotted us, maybe they will kill us."

[My son said], "My mother. If we ran to Thailand and if they spotted us, maybe they will kill us." After those eight years, we decided we couldn't go on like this anymore. They would find us one day or another. That's why my new husband decided to take my children and I to Thailand. We walked for 20 days. We were very hungry. We arrived on a mountain looking over the Mekong River. The Vietnamese followed us to the mountain, and they killed my second husband on that mountain, like they killed my first. My children and I were very scared. We ran and hid in the bushes for two days. We were starving. Then my son said, "My mother. If we ran to Thailand and if they spotted us, maybe they will kill us."

I told my son we should not go. "What if they kill us? You are still very young. You could not take care of us and cannot pull us [across the river]." And at that time, my son was 12 years old and my daughter was 13. And my second husband's daughter was four at that time.

I told my son we should not go because you are still young and small. You could not take us across the river. If they would try and kill us, you could not do anything. But then we came out anyway to the bank of the Mekong River. We were there for one day.

My son said, "Use the rope. Wrap it around your waist and I will try and pull you." He also said, "If we all get across, we will go on. If we all fail in the middle of the river, we all die together," because we were very scared of the Vietnamese. And when we got to the water, the Vietnamese did try to kill us once, but they did not hit us. My son swam and pulled us slowly across the Mekong River. He got us across to the other side.

When we got across, we looked back to the other side and we all felt very depressed. We cried very much, for we left our father and husband on that mountain. No one will bury my husband in the ground. We cried so much, looking over the Mekong River to the mountain.

The Thai people sent me to Camp Vannei. I stayed there for six months. I missed my son very much. The Americans loved us very much, so they came to interview us and give us a way to come to this country. Maybe our father is in America, too. Maybe he was there already. So we had to go and look for him in America.

I was very depressed. When we were in the camp, two of my daughters were growing up. So my daughter and I followed my son to America. And even though we got there, we couldn't find their father anywhere.

When we were in Thailand, we thought that our father was in America. But when we got here, we still couldn't find our father. I asked all around for my husband and no one could find him. I was very deeply in grief, and very depressed. But my son had come to America and he had grown up to be a young man. So now my son is over 16 years old and I think that he can help me, and he is why some of my tears have stopped.

When I arrived in this country, all the American people loved me very much, too. I am not so poor anymore and my heart has settled down a little bit — and so have my tears. I have found a friend, an American friend. She is a lady like me. She loves me very much. She helps me very much. I didn't have clothes to wear, so she helped me with clothes to wear. And people have loved me very much.

I feel very sorry for myself and for the grief that I have. But this friend of mine is very special, and she loves me very much. I am very happy to have her. It's like having my mom and dad. Having her love and help me feels like my mom and dad have risen again. And I am very happy again. It makes my heart, that is very depressed and cries so much, brighter. I am very happy that she helped me so much. It makes me feel like I still have a way of living in this country. People in America are very kind to me. They helped me very much. That's why my tears have stopped running for a little bit, and I am happy that my son has grown up and he can help me.

I am very depressed that I don't have a relative. I don't have a parent. I feel that in the whole world, they give me all the grief and let me get poor and depressed, all for me to carry. I cried so often looking up in the sky and begging for my happiness and love, asking the sky for help. I got to this county. It was very good for me. Many people helped. But just one thing remained; I didn't have a husband to help teach my children. I wanted to tell all about my grief, my poverty, to the world.

Pa Lee's daughter holds her baby at a welcoming ceremony.
Sandra Shackelford Collection, University of Wisconsin-Green Bay, Archives Department.

My name is Pa Lee. I am 57 years old. My grief, my guilt and my tears. Anger. My hunger. The only person in the world that has this much grief, just let me be the one.

My heart, my lungs, melting, crying, looking over the world, seeing if the world would love me and leave me my life. I don't know who to tell my grief to. No husband. No parents. No relative. No one to love. Crying.

I pray for the world to tell my grief to and to have it written down as a story for my children. For them to say, this grief is told by Pa Lee and the whole world has given her the grief to carry over her shoulder. To tell the world and all the people that the only person that is so depressed and has so much grief, is Pa Lee. And let her be the only one in the world to have a story to tell her children, grandchildren, family and friends. To tell them that Pa Lee is the one that has a broken heart. My heart and my lungs cry, melting in my eyes. To know that I am very poor and very sad. It is so sad that it looks just like the rain comes with a windstorm to this world. That is all I have to say.

Thor Xiong smiling.
Sandra Shackelford Collection, University of Wisconsin-Green Bay, Archives Department.

Thor Xiong (Thao Chang)

You were born in Laos 60 years ago. How many brothers and sisters do you have?

They are younger than me. One brother is younger. And the other, two. Aunt Ber and Yer [or Zer], [these are Thao Chang's sisters]. We are from the same father. And there are five sisters. Three brothers. And there's one brother. He went to be a soldier. The Vietnamese shoot him and his wife in the war. Except the oldest uncle and the youngest uncle. [Once we marry, we call the brothers 'uncle'.] The oldest uncle had died in 1989. And right now, I just have the youngest uncle.

Thao Chang, how old were you when you got married?

I was 25 [years old.]

What was your husband's name?

My husband's name is Cher Khou Chang.

And you had your son. What was his name?

He is called Pao Ge.

How did your husband die?

I think it was the year 1964, on December 4th. He went back to other country [Laos] and the Vietnamese killed him. He has a sister-in-law over there. He went to visit her and bring her over, but the Vietnamese caught him and killed him. He never came back to us.

How old were you and your son then?

My son? I just giving birth to him. And he's about three or two months old. Then my husband died.

How did you find out that he was dead?

They came from there [Laos]. When he left [us] was the first [of the month]. He got there and he died on the fourth [of the month].

And you just had a baby? You had to be terrified?

I don't remember being scared or terrified. God loves us. And I wasn't terrified.

You have a lot of faith in God.

That's right!

Let's talk about your childhood. Why can't you remember any happy thing? Was there always war?

I don't know what to think then. There's always run and run. And scared and scared.

So that's how your childhood was spent? Running?

When I'm young, the country was still good until when I got to be a teenager. We always ran from war. Ran from place to place — from Phou Houa to Ba Peng, from Ba Peng to Muang Cha. When we got to Muang Cha then we run back to Ba Peng. Then the Vietnamese came, and we ran back to Muang Ong.

We lived in Muang Ong. When I lived in Muang Ong my child was about this tall (demonstrates) and knew how to talk. We lived there for one rice season. Then I was doing one rice season with my uncle, Chang [clan's last name]. Then they sold their rice land, and they ran away. Then I was back eating with my mother. They went and we lived there.

I don't know why, but God loves me very much. I lived in Ban Naphia, and I didn't get hurt. Then I was out of here and went to live over there. And then the Vietnamese came and I wasn't hurt either.

Then, in 1978, I live in town and both of my uncles [brothers] were farming over there. Then I was very scared, and I said to myself (humming), "Now my mother died and I'm deaf. What if they run from the war and they didn't tell me?" Then I didn't have faith in God yet. But I had prayed [to] Heaven that "I am very deaf. Would you please love me, too?" If they ran away and they don't tell us, what if my son and I wake up and the Vietnamese are all over? What am I going to do? Then I ask God to help. At the time, both of my brothers went to get their rice. After they finished doing the rice, we moved here to there. We went about five days and the Vietnamese were shooting. "*Pe Pong.*" [Bang. Bang] from the other side at us. But at first, during the war *Kong Lia* [The Japanese War] my mom stayed at home. I was at the farm. Gun was goin thong! thong! thong! boom! boom! boom!

Oh, my heart just couldn't stay still. Why was there the gun sound all over at home? They kept going and going. And later, everybody was running over there. I can't believe it. I am happy that God really loves me.

Wherever I live, I didn't get hurt. Nothing! (Tho Chang laughs.) Happy. And believe that God is the One that really loves me. Even though I can't hear anything and I'm deaf in this world, God still loves me. And when we were running to Moung Cha, the Vietnamese came to Ban Naphia. I was in the farm and they [the people] ran after me, too [because the Vietnamese soldiers were shooting]. (laughs) I wasn't hurt at all!

Wherever I go, I don't feel scared. When we left, the Vietnamese lied to my brothers that they killed us and they got both of us [both Thao Chang and her son]. "They both died. We killed them." My youngest sister and brother of my sister, they were crying for me. They told us that, before you came, they said you both died and your people cried a lot for you both. Because they said the Vietnamese killed you both. But they went and took a look at the dead people. None of them were us. Not our bodies. Maybe we got over. Even wherever we go, it's always good. People that come, the ones that got killed by the Vietnamese or got hurt and died, they are all over. The one in back got hurt and the one in front of us also got hurt. We weren't that scared. The Hmong people that were just passing us, they got killed, too. I'm just happy that God helped us and there's nothing to compare it with.

Thao Chang, tell me one time God was taking care of you. One very dangerous time.

You don't know — when I was young and single, we went to the New Year festival. We were tossing the ball and there was no war yet. But that day they were shooting guns. They were shooting, shooting, and that gun noise stopped long, like when you were here. When the sun goes down, there was a bullet that came right in front of my head and fell down right in front of me. And I was all right. (laughs again) I'm very surprised. It was God that helped me.

Is it a time of war? Why were they shooting?

No! There was a boy in the Army that was home. And I guess he was trying to show them how to fire a gun. The gun noise had stopped for a long time, but that bullet flew right in front of me and I didn't get hurt. Then I told my boyfriend to come here. "You come here and I'll tell you something. I've got something here. "He ran to me, and I gave him that warm bullet right in his hand. And he ran over to the people that were shooting. (laughs)

Thao, when did you lose your hearing?

I think I was ten years old when my ears started hurting. My ears hurt and then I couldn't hear, and that's when I couldn't hear anymore.

When you were running with your new baby, how did you run with him? Did you carry him?

I fed him breast milk. When I breast fed him, I tried to eat a little bit so he got breast milk. When I started running, I carried food, rice, on my back. I was running with my mother's [family]. They helped me, too. The time I get very tired they help me. When he was bigger, I just put him on top of my basket [on my back] and just went.

How did you get to the camp, and which camp did you go to?

I first stayed in camp Nong Khai. Then we went to Vannei. We got there in September. We stayed there until December, and then we came over here.

When we came from the other side, it was very difficult. When we came from the head of the river, the water was not too deep. But when we got to the end, it is about this deep (demonstrates the depth of the water with her hand). And then, when we left there, we took the one that goes up, that's very big! When we get to the head of it, it's very small. When you're in the water, you're not afraid of the mines. But when you go inland, you're afraid of the mines. So we just stayed walking in the water. When you're in the water a long time, your skin gets wrinkled.

When we arrived, some of the water was about this high. My child was still small, but he said, "Mom. Let me hold you." But I told him, "My son, you cannot hold me. Let me get a stick to hold on to it first before we go because this water is very deep." Nobody helped us to hold our hand. And I just held on to this stick.

After we passed that river, people passed us. Nobody helped us. We came to look for a place to sleep. Nobody helped make houses. There was some woman that doesn't have a house or place to sleep. When we were asleep, they just crawled in behind us.

We trucked for 13 days, then we reached Mont Phou Houa. When we were there, we were very, very hungry. Our eyes were blurry — we couldn't see anything. My child was smaller and he could see better, so I told the boy to go and look for roots – of yam – and find a vine so I could dig for us. Then he'd go and find a dry vine and I would go and dig for the roots for us to eat. There was a man. His last name is Yang. By the name of Shoua Chai Yang. Whenever he dug up yam roots, he always gave my son some. I will never forget his kindness.

> Whenever he dug up yam roots, he always gave my son some. I will never forget his kindness.

I think right now he lives in St. Paul. But I don't know if he is alive or dead. Whenever I dig up some roots, I always gave some to him and when he got some, he gave some to my son. And so we all survived. I would eat the raw side and leave him the ripe side [the core]. We were very, very hungry then.

> **The Hmong said that I should sell my earrings. They lied to me that, if you keep that on and you get to the river and cross it, there will be dragon that will drown you.**

The Hmong said that I should sell my earrings. They lied to me that, if you keep that on and you get to the river and cross it, there will be dragon that will drown you. I said, "Why are you lying to me? My gold earrings came from the water. It didn't come from anywhere. Gold came from the water and I'm not going to be afraid. And I think this is the one that is going to save my life and I won't sell it." Then I just use the decoration part of the earrings to buy some salt. Then it leaves me the earring.

We were still hungry. The Laos came. They looked at us. They said they won't let us have anything and then we both cried. They looked at us and it looked like they loved us too. And they said, "Do you have any relatives in Thailand?" Then I say, "Yes we do." Because we sent over one silver bar and that's why, when we came, the Laotians helped us. They said that I should swim across because I do not have enough money. I said, "How could I? I don't know how to swim in the water. You have to help me."

They helped us because we were crying. And they took us across the river. Then we came to Nong Khai. We stayed there for a couple of days and then we got our pass to stay in the camp. We got there and we lived there for one year. Then we went to Vannei. We got to Vinai and then made our name and we got interviewed. After they interviewed us, I don't know but I have a dream that said, "Here's your number. You must remember 444243." And when our name is up, the same number came up. It is like God taught us. (laughs).

When you said they wouldn't let you cross, who said that?

It was the Laotian people. They told me that, but the reason they let me cross in the boat is because I sent one silver bar ahead. And I had my other gold earring so I gave them that, too. When we got there, I went and got that silver bar to give to them. That is why we got away.

Who had your silver bar? Was it your relatives in Thailand?

Yes. It was the relative in Nong Khai that had kept it for me.

What did you have left when you got to the camp? Did you have anything left when you got to the camp?

I had my son and I left!

Thao Chang, when did you come to the U.S.?

December 1979.

Did you come right to Green Bay, or did you go to another city first?

We got to Chicago. We had a sponsor that's about her [Sandy's] age. We lived with her for eight months until my sister, Yer, came. Then we went to live with her until they said they're going to cut down our funds [welfare payments] because we lived with my sister. Then we moved out of my sister's house to live by ourselves. We lived by ourselves about four years. Then we moved to Eau Claire. And then I applied for SSI. I got that. Then my sister took me here, to Green Bay, in 1986.

Thao Chang, I met you when you came to our senior class. You were very small and very quiet. It didn't take me long to see how smart you were. Did you ever go to school?

When I was small, I never went to school. But people who knew me when I was young, they said I was very talkative.

Where did you learn to read and write English?

When I lived in Chicago. I studied for five years. That's why I know a little bit.

You are so funny! We have a joke about you whether you are in class or not! We say, if you were with us, you are the leader! You are always out in front of everyone and you never get lost. How did you get like this?

> I could remember places very good. Wherever I go, I know I will not get lost. I go there, go there, come back and find you guys! (laughs heartily)

I only have a few more questions. You are about to go to North Carolina. You are about to leave all of your friends. You have to do what your son tells you. How do you feel about this?

> Well, when I go there, my son has raised a lot of chickens. So I think I'm going to help him with that and help him take care of his children.

I have one more question. This is a question for the whole world. What kind of world would you like it to be? If you could make the world any way you would want it to be, how would you make it?

> I think I wish everybody would love each other in the world and there would be no gangs. One doesn't kill another. Because a couple of weeks ago, there was some gang who killed a young American boy and I loved him very much, even though I don't know him. I feel very sorry for him. When I saw him on TV, I loved him very much. Why would a person like that have to be killed? In this world there are too many wars going on like this. Regardless if it's Hmong or American. Whoever got killed, I love them very much.
>
> I think there's a red car here that belongs to him [the boy who was killed]. After he died, nobody touched it. When I see this car, I love him very much. I think if he didn't die, he would drive this car. Why would he die and leave his car there and not be driven? Maybe this world has so much freedom and that's why there is all this war and killing.
>
> There are thieves and killing people in the house. We live by our own and live by themselves. Why would they have to kill? That day, I walked here to there and I came back at five o'clock, which is still early. I don't know why they closed Maple Street on both sides.

I don't know. I went over and I said to myself, "Why are so many people there? Why are there so many police cars? What is going on here?" I walk down the street. There are so many reporters and people who take movies all over the street. People are all over and I think maybe they had taken that dead person out already. They took one lamp and one sofa into a truck. Maybe that's because this world looks like this. I have a friend living close to me. I told her that I love her very much. "Just because I can't understand your language and you don't understand mine. I am going to leave you. But I love you and when I miss you, I will write to you." This is all I have to say. And even though I say it backward to forward, and even though I live here, I didn't have anything to say to you to listen.

As we conclude the interview, Thao Chang adds this:

The other day, the guy upstairs and the guy downstairs, they had grilled some meat and they had no rice to eat with it. I asked them if they wanted some rice. And they said, "Yes." Then I got a bowl of rice and bring it to them.

A Deaf Woman's Prayer

Thor Xiong

My name is Thor Xiong. I lived in Laos, and my husband died early. I am very poor but I'm still alive to work and support my son. We were running from the war. We were with the Hmong people, and they didn't love us at all. But God loves us, and we are still alive. We were running from the war and when we started from the end of the river, it was very small and [then] it became wider, until you couldn't even see cross it. We were going down toward the end of the river and the river gets so deep that you cannot go in. My grief is as big as this.

We were making a house for us, and we had only other Hmong people, and they didn't help us at all. When we came out to Mount Phou Houa Law, Hmong people didn't help us. The Hmong killed two big animals from the forest, and they were fighting [over the meat]. They were very poor, too. They came and lived beside us. Then we came and we were all very poor. We didn't have anything, and our clothes were all torn. But we were still alive. Then we reached Thailand, and the Thai people even asked me to sell my child.

But I told them, "I only have one son and if I sold him, how would I live without him? I couldn't live and I can't do that." So, they didn't say anything. When we got to Nong Khai [the camp], we were very poor. There's nothing to compare it to. But God loves us. We were still alive and strong. We got to this country, and we started to believe in God. And we are now living like other people because of the love of the government. And I thank God. In my past life, since my Mom and Dad had me, we were very poor. My dad died when I was very small. We were very poor. There was nothing. Nobody to love us. Just God to love us and keep us alive. While running from the war, I found that I am deaf. What if the communists came and all the people left? And they did not wait for me? But God still let me be the first to run and the first to find the head way. When I found the way, I was not that poor anymore. God loves me and even though I am deaf, He still loves me and let me live. We got to America. I want to tell you all about that. When I live in Laos, I was very poor, but I don't know if God spoke to me. When I went to sleep at the rice field, I saw two stars holding hands, coming over to this [the American] side.

I was very sad and poor. I said, "Oh, God. I wish my son and I could be just like those stars and leave this behind." All of a sudden, it was going just like that. So I thought God is the One that showed me and He's the One that opens the way. Maybe He loves me because I am deaf and He let me be alive. I came to see freedom. I am very happy. And thank you, God. And I want to thank you all, the government, for taking me into this country. Even though my child went and married an American wife, I am happy that she is a child of the people of this country. I have nothing that I am sad or disapproving of because I think that the Americans will love my son. Wherever he goes, the Americans will help him and love him like I thought. I want to thank you, God. I will never forget Him and there is nothing that is going to compare. I was very poor. Nobody loved me. I just cried and cried, tears falling down, and then I had to wipe off the tears and just go. Those hand-grenades exploded all over and we were very scared. Yet there was nothing that hit us. God opened the way for us to go.

God opened the way for us to go.

Lots of people come and cannot go through. But my son and I were with other Hmong people. We came and we passed through. Thank you, God, for God's love that still loves me and my son. Other people come and they fell. Branch sticks stuck them and got infected, and their shins got all scratched. But my son and I came, and nothing happened to us.

One Hmong man came, and he got scratches all over his shin and it got all infected, so he overdosed on opium. But we got through. Why, it looks like God is the one that loves us. I believe that He loves me and got me to this country to have freedom and to have love for my grief and poverty. And I thank you, God, and all of the government. And thank you Sandy. Sandy still loves me very much. And that's all I have to say.

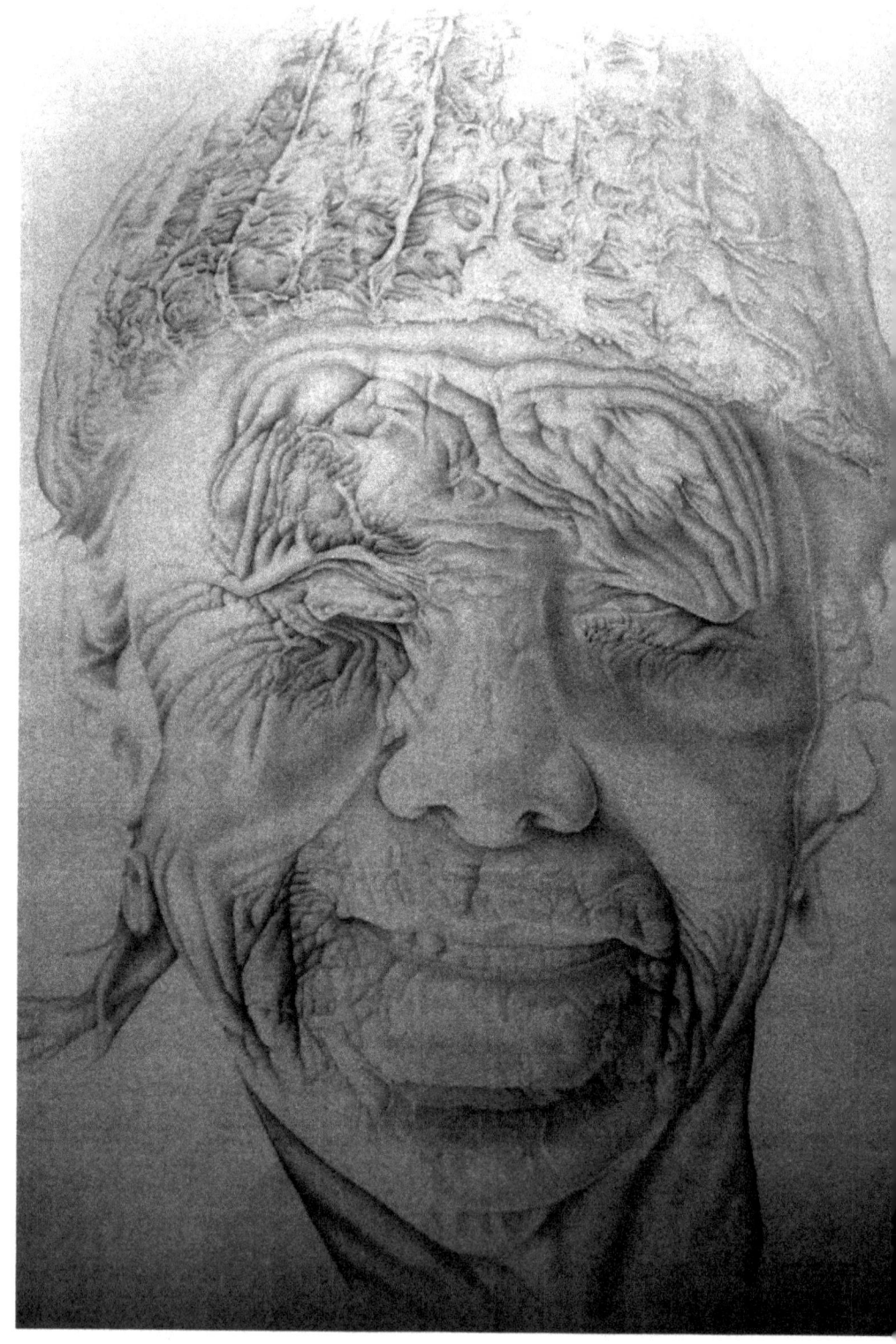

MAI XIONG

Sandra's drawing of Mai Xiong. Pencil on paper.

Mai Xiong

Mai, How old are you?

I am 120 years old.

A long time ago when [there was] the Hmong "crazy war," I was a young lady then. My mother took me to the farm and my father, the French took them [her father and her sisters] to Xiengkhouang Province. That was the first time the French ever came to Laos. They take my father and that was the French War.

How old were you then?

I think I was either 13 or 14.

Tell me the name of your village and what country you come from.

When the "crazy war" started, we live in Pan Hai Mong Ka to Hou Yu Hou Pan long bridge that's close to Moung Pa Muang Nham. I was born in Moung Pa Muang Nham in Laos.

When you were a little girl, what did your mother and father do?

When I was little and the "crazy war" started, we live in a small village. People were running to stay in the forest and in the farm. There was a big village and those people that live there, they go crazy.

(This is the French Indochina War. The following is Mai's description of how a certain group of people seeking power attempted to prove their superiority.)

They would put whole raw eggs in the rice smasher there and they would smash them. If the egg doesn't break, then they think they are not crazy. My mom and dad are just regular farm people. They farm for a living.

How many people were in your family?

I have two brothers, three [older] sisters, and one younger sister. When the French took three of them, they were scared, and they take medicine and opium to kill themselves. That left only one, with me.

What did you do as a little girl?

When I was a little girl, I helped my mother and father farm, cut poppy stems, and build soil around the roots of the poppy plant.

What was the crop you raised?

We plant rice and corn also because we live in the country and there was no government.

There has to be a planting of rice and a harvesting. How did you harvest the rice?

When we harvest the rice, we use a round knife. The Hmong call it "lia". They cut it and stack them this high (Mai Xiong demonstrates). And then we went and smashed it. After we smash them, we carry them and put them in a rice crib.

Do you remember your village when you were a little girl?

We lived in Houa Phanh, which is really a very hilly village. It's on a hill and down there. It's flat and over here it is our rice field, and we live on a hill. So that's our village on the hill. And way down there, there's a poppy field and rice field.

Right now, this place is still there. If I was there, I would still remember.

You were 14 years old when the French took over. What do you remember of that period when you were 14?

When the French came to our town, they just came to take people. They take everybody down the mountain called Pa Ling. When we got there, my mother took me and my brother... he's older than me. We ran to our poppy farm and the others, the French took them to Xieng.

They got my father and three sisters that I said had died. When they took the people down, they had put a rock pole and tied one person here and one person there. My father told us that when he got away.

Of all the people that they captured, they killed them. They said they killed them in Xieng but we don't know where in Xieng.
My father carried my little brother on his back. And the French had put red material on them. They said in three days they will kill them but there was a Chinese man that came and rescued them [all of the people]. So all the Hmong people got away.

That Chinese man come and said, "Whoever did not do wrong, you should let them go." So they let all the women, children and all the Hmong people go. I don't know where he came from, but he spoke Hmong and he was Chinese.

Why would they kill people in the first place? What did they do?

The only wrong thing was what they called the "crazy war". They kept saying stuff. They kept saying there will be a new king and they will take over the world. And I don't know why, but they killed the Laotian people. But not all the Hmong, just some of them.

So when the French come, they just take everybody because they said all the Hmong are crazy.

How did you feel when your sisters died?

(Here Mai Xiong contradicts herself, saying she is oldest, second oldest.)
We were very scared. Everybody was running away. We ran away to the farm with my mother and for a long time then we heard they [her sisters] died. A lot of people got taken away. Everybody, all the Hmong people, were taken.

I was very scared. I think that if they catch me, then they are going to kill me. I cried. But you know, my sisters, they were all prettier than me. They don't look like me.

How did the French occupy your village? What happened **next?**

After that, the French didn't come anymore because the Chinese man helped us. We lived in our village farm and did what we were all supposed to do, and there was no French anymore.

14 years old. 15 years old! What happened next in your life?

It was a long time after that. After my father came back, he told us to build new homes and find new lands for farming. So all we did was get homes built and we farmed. We harvested for a living. It's been a long time. I don't remember how many years after that. But after my father died, we buried him and then my mother, and we left.

We moved to Kham Pa Moung Ta. We lived there and I got married there. I got married after my father died. I was married to my husband, Hmong Vang, and then came the war and he died. Then I married my husband Hmong Moua. I have two children from my first husband when he died. He died after four years and the fifth year, I was married to my second husband, Hmong Moua. He was a soldier. The first one was not a soldier. I then moved to live in Xieng.

How did your first husband die?

He was sick and died. He was sick from his stomach to his chest and then he died. He was sick for one day and one night and then he died.

Mai, I'm sure you were beautiful. How did you marry? Did he take you on a date?

He came to marry me in my house. He asked my father to marry me in the Hmong traditional way. He was not really handsome. He is just like everybody else. (points to the interpreter.) I think he's a little taller than you.

How old were you when you got married?

I don't know. When the Japanese came, my first husband died, and I had two children then. That was the Japanese War. I don't know how old I am then, but last year I went to California and my brother's son showed me his father's birth paper and he was 135 years old.

My brother's name is Zang. He's the one that grew up with me nursing at our mother's breast. And that's the father of the nephew that lives in California. He's my older brother. When he showed me that his father is 135 years old, that's how I found out that I am 120 years old.

Did the Japanese come to take over your country?

When the Japanese came, we lived far away in the country. I don't know. Japanese came to Xieng and we just heard about it. They came to Thathom Tal Vien. We hadn't seen them. And we didn't know what they were there for. All we know is that the Japanese came.

Nothing happened to disturb your life? How did you meet your second husband? How was life like for you and this husband?

He came and asked my brother because I was a widow then. So we just had to make one dinner, for my brother. And after that, then I come and live in Xieng with my husband, and my husband was a soldier, a red soldier, and that was the French soldier.

When we came, my husband was very poor. He got monthly money, but only 300 a month. So I came and I bought a home for us to live. I got a house for 10,000.

We lived there for two years and the third year, we used 20,000 to build another one [house] and we bought that land for 17,000. No. It's 70,000.

How did your husband serve the French?

He was always in the barracks on watch. The only time he came home was to eat and to visit us once in a while. The house and everything else, I took care of it. In the garden, I planted coffee and then I planted peaches, apples, and pears. The coffee, it takes three years to get ready.

Mai, tell me about the weather, the growing season.

When you plant fruit, that you can sell for money. I plant fruit, beans, and vegetables. I have many friends, so I put them at the store and my friends sell them for me. The earth is just right for planting. Not very cold and not very hot. I lived just outside Xieng and there are stores in Xieng. There's a lot of Laotians and there are Chinese people and Indian people that come and sell things, too.

How many children did you have at this time?

I have two daughters. One now lives in Milwaukee and one in Wausau. And one daughter that lives here. That's my first husband, Hmong Vang's daughter. (*Mai speaks now of the woman I just met.*) It was my daughter-in-law that came here. She is my daughter-in-law.

My first husband's son, he died because he was a soldier. And there is no son left. He was a soldier for General Vang Pao.

What did he do for the CIA?
(*Mai has not said he was in the CIA, the interpreter has.*)

He was a soldier for Xeng Lor. I think he was a lieutenant.

Where was this, Mai?

My son died in Xieng in Nong Het. At the time, I was living in Xieng where I bought my house and the land. My son just went out to be a soldier for General Vang Pao, and they were in Nong Het where they were killed by the Vietnamese [communists]. Nong Het is way over there. The French had lots of jobs. My husband was a captain. He taught the soldiers and walked three days to Muang Mahm to see the road, to see if there was any Vietnamese coming.

Gone all the time. Did not get rest. Husband go and go.
After that, they go from Nong Het to Pa Doung to Pa Khao. Then I went with Phanas Toubee and Tou Lia to Vientiane to live with them there. Then my husband come and married his second wife over there. After he married, I don't know how he [went and he] died.

Mai Xiong and her grandaughter.

How did your husband die? Was he sick or what happened?

He was killed in the war. They killed him. We never got him home. Never found him.

How did you know that your husband got killed?

I know because when the camp broke, the soldiers called me and told me that we have a very big fight. "We can not find your husband, the captain. We think he die." At the time, I live in Longcheng. When he did, it was not the French war. It was Vang Pao's war.

When you said they called, do you mean they used a telephone?

They use the walkie talkie and they call to the airport and one of his soldiers came and told me that, "Last night they fought all night and [they] cannot find him." I could not remember what year it is but it was just before we ran away from Longcheng.

I was married to him for a very long time. He went and died at the village Ban Na in the mountains there. He left me with two little kids. I cried very much and I'm very sad so I don't know how long ago.

What did you do next?

I didn't do anything. I have my two kids and I didn't take anything like my household stuff. I just leave them all. So I give 1,500 for them to take us to Phas Khes. Then we went to Song Li and to... I don't remember the name. We live there in the country.

(Interpreter asks: Did Vang Pao leave yet at that time? Mai answers: No. Vang Pao did not leave yet. He left the second time that Longcheng were down broken.)

Mai, did war come to your village?

No, it didn't come. But as soon as we heard shooting, we ran away because my husband went with the soldiers and left us with the French. I then moved to KhamHom and live there. I went back to pick my coffee. It was ready. Then I had sold them for 7,000 kip. Then the Vietnamese [communists] came. So did Thao Fou and Fai Dang. They said that we should not go away. They will not shoot us.

Did you hide in the mountains?

We went by foot into the forest through the mountains.

How many times did you have to move with your family?

So many times, I cannot count. We have been to Phou Khoun and Phouvieng. Phou Khoun is very high. We came for three nights to get there to Phou Khoun, Phouvieng because that's the very high mountain. My husband was still in Pa Doun. He did not come with us. It was my son-in-law that take us there. Then Phanas Toubee and Tou Lia, they heard that I live there so they came and took me to Vientiane. We were related because they married to my sister's cousin. I was still a shaman then. I have not come to God yet.

I lived in Vientiane for four to five years before I went to Longcheng. When I was in Longcheng, my husband married to the second wife but I did not think anything [of it]. I just want someone to care for him so I didn't mind. I am not mad.

Was Vientiane a large city?

It was like New York!

What was life like there?

It was very hot in Vientiane. I can't stand it. And there [were] a lot of mosquitos. They bite very much. I don't want to stay. I really like to go back home but I can't. The Americans have built some apartments for the refugees to stay in so we each live in one unit and they send us food.

Was it peaceful there at the time?

It was peaceful there at the time. It is very hot but there is no war because there was a lot of Laotians there.

Was it occupied by the U.S.?

No. It is not. But the U.S. help with food.

What year was it?

Oh, I don't know. It was very long after that. I was there for four years. The fifth year I went to live in Longcheng. I live with a lot of people. They sell stuff. But I have a garden and I was doing my crop at home. I don't know what years that was. We were there then my husband die. Then people move to Pon Ta and move back to Longcheng.

How long did you live in the capital?

I was there for five years and then I went back to live with my husband and his second wife in Long Cheng. They went to fight the war and he die. (Laughs in irony). It was funny to me because my second wife's life was very hard. I said, "That's what happens when you follow the husband very much!"

Mai, when did your journey to the United States begin?

People have left. We moved to Muang Ka to Nam Pha. Then we stay there and do farming. It was not good land to do farming. We went through wheat to farm. We were there for a couple seasons of crops. Then the Vietnamese come and then we ran back to Muang Om. We stay there until they ask us to go back. Then we come back and my daughter and son-in-law help us because they were in Thailand first and they got some money from him. So we came and the Vietnamese fight and they break [separate] my daughter that lives in Wausau and I from my daughter's family. We then go with a lot of Hmong. Then we didn't get to cross the river so we went back to stay with the Hmong and the Vietnamese people. I think it was about ten years.

I can't live there anymore because I am a soldier's wife. If they capture me, they will kill all the soldier's family.

I can't live there anymore because I am a soldier's wife. If they capture me, they will kill all the soldier's family. So I decided to come [to the U.S.]. When I got halfway, we were lost again. I stayed with the Hmong and they took all my money. But I had a lot of Laotian friends and they give me money to pay for the boat to Thailand. When I got to Thailand, I have no money so the Thai government said that the widow should get some money. So they each give like 20 or 30 baht. So I got 70 baht to make the paper stay in the refugee camp.

How long did you stay in Thailand?

I stayed about three or four months.

Was it a difficult journey?

Yes. The Laotians take us at night to cross the big river. First we crawl very slow and careful. Then they bring the boat out and we got in the boat and they take us across. I have to pay 12,000 kip to the boatman for me and my daughter,

Were you afraid?

Yes! Very scared. We just pray and came.

How long did you stay in Thailand, Mai?

Not very long. We were there when they got the rice planted until when the rice was ready to cut. Then we came to this country. It was in June. My little daughter came with my son-in-law's family to Thailand and when I got to Ban Vinai, I got my daughter back.

So my older daughter left to the U.S. with her family leaving me with my two girls. I think we were there for almost a year.

We were very poor and it was very hard for me. But we were very lucky. We got to Bangkok. We were there for two nights. They give us food to eat and we each eat a little bit and, all of a sudden, they said, "Here comes the plane!" And we got to the plane.

We got to St. Paul [Minnesota] because my son-in-law and he sponsor us. They love me as much as their mother because they have no mother and I have help them a lot in the past. We were there for one week and then my daughter got married. Then moved to Wausau and then we move there. We stay there until I move here [in Green Bay]. Both of my daughters got married. Then the relative that live here came and took me to Green Bay to stay with them and with my older daughter here.

Do you like living in Green Bay, Mai?

Yes, I like to stay because I can't go anywhere else, but I want to stay here.

What was the most frightening part of your journey?

I am not scared in this country. But in Laos, there was war and I am very scared. In here, just a little bit. At night when I sleep, because I live alone, I'm just afraid people might get in and rob me, even though I don't have anything. But whenever somebody knocks on my door, I always ask. If I don't know them, I don't open the door.

Do you have a garden here, Mai?

No. I don't have one. But my daughter, Mrs. Chong Houa Kong, have one and I go with her to help her.

What do you enjoy most about this country? What do you like the best?

In this country, I like to grow my own fruit and flowers because in Laos I do that all the time. I would go water the plants and watch them grow. I do that all day long.

> In this country, I like to grow my own fruit and flowers because in Laos I do that all the time.

How do you like winter in Wisconsin?

I can't do anything, just stay home and watch television. I like the cold better than California.

What is your favorite television program?

I like to watch cowboy shows because they show all the mountains and it reminds me of Laos.

In your 120 years you have seen so much, Mai, what do you think about today's young people?

I like it more here. The young people have a better living here. They just stay and work. They don't have to do very hard work like in our country. We work very hard. We walk up and down the hill. Carry heavy on our back. It is very good in this country.

Mai and her herb garden.
Sandra Shackelford Collection, University of Wisconsin-Green Bay, Archives Department.

How does it feel to leave your homeland? What do you miss most about it?

I miss it. I miss my home. I miss my stuff in the garden.

Was it hard to leave your homeland?

Yes. I flew to the U.S. I am very poor when I got here.

How was it when you came to the U.S.?

I came with my daughter walking.

When you walked to Thailand, how many miles did you walk?

We came walking through the jungle. The woods because we were afraid of the Vietnamese and there's no car. It took me 15 days to reach Thailand.

Were you afraid?

Yes. I was afraid and if I am not lucky, I would have been killed. Thank God for helping me.

Was there fighting going on?

You can not stay still because guns would go off and on and there are bombs all over. I am a soldier's wife so I was on the run all the time because they would look for me all the time.

Did you have close calls?

My husband have always been a soldier ever since the French came. Then when the Americans came, he also work for them.

How did you get the money together to come to the U.S.?

I don't have much. The money was robbed by the Laotians that become Vietnamese communists. So I don't have any at all. They took all of my money. I don't have any at all. Just get help from the Thai people for rice and food.

Did they help you pay for your airline ticket to the U.S.?

Yes, they paid for them all because I am the wife of a soldier. The government of the U.S. helped me.

What was the scariest thing about being on an airplane?

I was not scared because I was poor and wanted to leave.

What do you think of coming to the United States?

I am happy now. I don't want to go back because over there, they are very bad [the communists]. And it's very poor there.

Mai, how do you enjoy your days?

I can't do anything because I'm too old and I can't see very good. Even if I want to do it, I'd need glasses so I don't do it.

Are you 120 years old?

Yes. I am 120 years old.

If you could make a wish for all the people, what would it be?

I don't have anyone in Laos anymore. I think if I could still see very good and if somebody needs help, I would like to help them. I'm getting old. Very forgetful. I leave stuff laying around. I forget where I put it.

What do you think about war?

I'm very scared. I don't want to see it anymore. I hate it. And I'm very scared. I don't want any more war.

Do you think there will be a time when there will never be war again?

I don't know. I can't say it.

Mai's family.
Sandra Shackelford Collection, University of Wisconsin-Green Bay, Archives Department.

Mai holding a portrait of a relative.
Sandra Shackelford Collection, University of Wisconsin-Green Bay, Archives Department.

The Healer

Mai Xiong

Mai in her living room.
Sandra Shackelford Collection, University of Wisconsin-Green Bay, Archives Department.

(The following interview took place after Mai Xiong moved to an apartment adjacent to her daughter's and family.)

My name is Mai Xiong. I saw her [Sandra] and I am very happy she came to see me today.

You have been my teacher, Mai. Would you help teach me again?

Yes.

You are a healer. How did you become a healer? How did you know you could help people?

When I was young, I didn't know. But my mother's sister-in-law was a healer. She knew all about herbs. When I had my first child and my mother died, after that I went and learned. I learned all the herbs.

In Laos before, those herbs cost 12 kip to learn them. And I did not learn just one thing. I learned many kinds. One: the herbs which heals a man's loosened colon that was moved outside his body and, in a woman, the urinary channel that has done the same thing.

Secondly, the kind that heals heartburn and chest pain that you have sharp pain through the back that hurts very bad. And the chest pain when you cough up blood. In this country they might say this is pneumonia or bronchitis. And many, many more. That's how I know.

Is this—your ability to heal with herbs—a special gift that some-one is given? Were you chosen to be a healer, or was it something you wanted to learn?

I chose to learn. These medicines are from learning. When they teach you, you know how. You go and pay money to the person that knows herbs very well. Then they teach you that this kind is good for this and that kind is good for that.

The herbs that heal people when they cough up blood. The cost of it could be one. If their food was poisoned and then they drink and eat it, they will not be sick at the same time but they start coughing, coughing and cough until they get a little red blood. They teach you all that kind of medicine.

Did you work with herbs? Did you grow them? What is the medicine made from?

All those herbs were in the forest. The kinds of herbs to give to people who could not have a baby. When I go learn that, they teach me that kind of medicine also. Now, all the people that I give the herbs to and have a baby, some live in France and some, I don't know where they are.

Mai's healing herbs.
Sandra Shackelford Collection, University of Wisconsin-Green Bay, Archives Department.

Do you remember what it was like to go out into the forest to gather herbs?

Very nice. Very beautiful. Many kinds of bushes. A lot of grass. Trees. You just take a walk through it. You could see them. The kind that heals the people that one side of the body doesn't work [a stroke]. This herb also grows in the forest in Laos. But it's a very big and tall tree that has white, long strings that hang down off the tree.

When you see those, you gather the white strings and use that to boil them and wash the side of the body that doesn't work with the boiled water and herb. Then the person can walk and get strength in his arms and legs again.

This medicine that you know, is it an ancient medicine?

Those medicines are not very old. But since I learned them, they are always there. They teach many kinds. There's a tree, or it looks like a tree. When the leaves fell, the leaves would stand up around the trunk of the tree. And every season that those leaves fell, the rhinoceros always ate them. It's the best kind of herbs for stroke but there is no more of those trees. In my country where we lived, it does not have it, too. It's very back in a city called Phouvieng and Phou Khoun and another place still has a few of them.

Did you ever run into a rhinoceros?

No. Those rhinoceros are not the same kind as the ones in this country. It doesn't just have two horns. Rhinos in my country have four horns — two on the side of the head, one on the top of the head and one growing from the forehead. Nowadays, no one has the rhinoceros' horn anymore. Maybe except my sister-in-law, Cher Pao, might. Or maybe she doesn't. If she doesn't, there is none. I don't think this country's rhinoceros is the real rhinoceros.

Does the rhinoceros horn have special healing powers?

Yes.

Does it heal?

The rhinoceros horn heals many things.

The rhinoceros horn heals many things. I had one rhinoceros' toenail when my grandfather shot it, but I lost it all at the river. We were coming over to Thailand and crossing the river. And I gave it to my daughter that was my stepdaughter. At the time, she was still small. And she lost it. I was lost with the other oldest daughter and my stepdaughter was crossing the river with someone else. And they were scared. And they told her to take off the sack she was carrying that the medicines were in. And she took it off and threw it away because the communists were shooting. And that's when I lost all my herbs. Not one left. Stuff that I brought from Laos was all lost in the river. I don't have any anymore.

What medicines were you bringing with you across the Mekong River?

My herbs of many kinds. The herbs for coughing up blood. That's one of them. Some of them for the baby when they get fever, when they get very hot and they get chicken pox or measles. All those herbs were lost. The herbs for the people who could not have a baby. And most important, the herbs for people that's sick and they passed out. I had all that and lost them all. We were going very far. We could not carry all of them. But I gathered a small bag, and the whole bag was lost when they took it off and threw it away.

Can you remember that day that you ran? Was it in the morning?

When we ran, it was very tragic. But if I say it, I could never be done saying it. We stayed and when General Vang Pao took off, we got halfway to Hin Heup. The people that were ahead of us, most of them got killed and we ran back. We lived there until the communists were going to kill us, then we ran again. We ran in the daytime. I don't know what day it was. What date it was. We were very scared. And the time that we ran, we ran to Phouvieng. I never had a baby [with my second husband]. The daughter in Wausau was the one that I picked up along the road. I raised her.

She had just been here and maybe this Saturday we're going to have a party and maybe they will come. The daughter in Milwaukee is my stepdaughter. When my husband died, she was only a year old, and I raised her also. My daughter has seven babies. She just had a little baby who is just starting to sit up — four sons and three daughters. The oldest granddaughter is ten years old. I don't know what to say. Everybody is running. The people that have husband, they have places to live. The three of us, we don't have a husband. We just follow the people and nobody makes places for us to live.

At night we just cut off banana leaves and cover ourselves. When it rained, we got all wet. Then I put my kids in front of me and used a plastic sheet to cover us. We just stayed and slept that way. It was very tragic.

Other people had husbands. At night they could build a little banana leaf house. The three of us — the girl is still very little — when we were going to come to Thailand, the oldest daughter was... I don't know what age. But at the time she knew how to go and pick vegetables already. The youngest one was still very young yet. The little one could just carry a little bag of rice. But the oldest one could help me carry blankets. Clothes. And I carry food, pots and dishes. We were very poor. No luck.

How do you think you survived? You have come such a long way.

You can't stay because you are a soldier's wife and if they find out, they will capture you because your husband was a colonel. We were running and running until my husband died. And if we stayed, your children and girls. And if they capture you, they are going to take your girls away and that's not good. That's why we got out and ran and tried to catch up with my oldest daughter. There were a lot of people. About one to 200 families running. We kept following them.

Do you think some spirit was watching over you?

I think God was watching over us. I think God helped us, too. When we came, there were a lot of people that had been killed and could not cross the river. We came and my oldest daughter's family and my family, we got to the river and they were shooting and everybody separated.

My oldest daughter and my youngest daughter went one

way. And my other stepdaughter and I went the other way. Because they got our rubber floats and we didn't have one so we went back to live with the Laotian people. We were caught by communists. They took all the money we had. We had 40,000 kip and they took it all. Also my daughter had a sash with 90 silver coins hanging on it, and they took that, too. They kept that. And they said, "We will not take it away. We will keep it here for you. But if you run away, you will never get it back."

We didn't have anything at all. But there was a Laotian lady that saw us and she loved us very much. She told me not to cry so much even though all my kids are gone. "If you want to go, I will send you," she said.

I didn't have any money but there was still 10,000 kip for the Laotian woman to send me across the river to Thailand. When we got there, I just came like this! We didn't have any money but our relatives in Thailand helped us until we got 75 baht so we could get our papers. Then they sent us to the camp until a month later before they sent us to Ban Vinai

When we got to Ban Vinai, I don't know how long we lived there. But my daughter was grown up then. It was the time that they had planted rice. The rice was ready to cut and we harvested it. That was about in June. That's when we interviewed to come to the United States. Our name came up and we came to the States.

You have come so far, Mai. You have come from Laos. You have lived a long life and have seen so much history. What do you think about your life?

I really want to go back. I miss the place. The country, very much. But I can't go back. In this country, there are no herbs. No medicine. We have to use the doctor's medicine. I know the herbs but there are none that grow in this country. Since we came, I miss my country very much. I said we wouldn't come to this country, but I was one of the soldier's wives and I think, even though my husband died, they might capture us and take my daughter away. They will leave me alone and I will be poor and get old. That's why we ran. We were very poor. No place to live. Nobody made a place for us. That's why I decided to come. People said, when you get to Thailand then you get to America. Because my oldest daughter was gone already. Their name came up first and they came first to the United States.

I think God helped me very much. I have no sins because I have done nothing wrong. So that's why we got the interview and that's why they didn't use my real age. If they used my real age, the kids wouldn't be able to come with me. That's why my age is younger than I am so I could take my daughters with me. My real age would have been 120 last year. They said that I was a soldier's wife so that is why I didn't have to pay air fare.

You are my family, Mai, and I am your family. You have changed my life and the lives of other people. I am grateful to you.

I love you the same as if you were my daughter and I am very happy to have you. I also have a friend that was American that lives at my old address. She often visited me but when she had her first baby, her husband took her away. They live somewhere far away now but she used to live next door to me. She loves me very much, too. Everything she eats, she shares with me. These couch covers came from her. When she had her baby, she brought the baby and stayed with me for a while when the baby was very small. After that the basement got flooded and the manager didn't fix it. Housing didn't pay and they asked me to move out. That's why I found this place. It has been a year now since I have seen her. She loves me as much as you. I haven't seen her ever since.

To me, you are like that small flower over there. You are beautiful and full of surprises.

I am very happy. Thank you. I miss the other lady very much until I met you and I know you. That's why I forget the other one because I don't know where she is anymore. I miss you very much and I love you as my daughter and I will love you until I no longer live.

Your words are full of wisdom.

I think I got to this country now and I don't think there is ever a way to get back to Laos again. You can't go back until the country is back to normal again and the government would send everyone back — then we would go. But if I don't live until that day, I will stay here.

Mai's healing medicines.
Sandra Shackelford Collection, University of Wisconsin-Green Bay, Archives Department.

Life in Camp

Nyoua Thao

I am Mrs. Za Ker Thao. I am going to say just a little bit to the American lady. She wants me to say more but I don't know what to say, so I will just say a little bit. I will talk about my life when my mom and my dad, Sengsue, gave birth to me. We lived poorly. We lived in Laos. We farmed for a living. This is what I have to say.

My dad had passed away early and left my mother. Mother was very poor. She stayed single for a while until she remarried and then lived with her uncle. Mom was alive for some time; then she, too, passed away.

We lived in Laos. We did not know how to do much to support ourselves but farm. We didn't know how to earn anything. We stayed in Laos until the Vietnamese came. Ye Sa La was mean to us. He came and every day he told threatening news to the people. The people were afraid, so they moved to Na Houa. When we reached Na Houa, we were very hungry because we never received the shipment of rice. Every day we went out to dig in the ground for yams of all sorts to eat. I will just say simply this much to you, American Aunt.

We came to live in Na Houa and later moved to Neen. Then we lived in Neen. They were mean to us there, too. The Vietnamese came and took my son and the teacher, Keu, away to Hou Sai for about one week. They said they were taking them to spread the word to Hou Sai. Our people went to check on them. It was about a week later when they were finally released.

The children were afraid, so they moved to Thailand and lived in Baton. We lived in Baton till they sent us to Nam Nyao. We lived in Nam Nya for three months until we went to Vinai. I will simply say this because I don't know how else to say it.

When we lived in Vinai, the Thai were also mean to us. The Thai plowed away hedges and cemeteries to make land and space for us to live on. Caskets were buried below us. The people like us were living on top of them. They plowed all the dead bodies to that area and covered them with land, creating a landscape for us to settle on. This is what I have to say.

The houses standing above the dead bodies were made of metal. One sheet right after another. At night it would seem like somebody was walking, touching the walls, walking back and forth from one end of the camp to the next. But when you got up to check, there was no one there. You came back in to sleep and it would start up again. Some days, when it was nice out, you woke up and it sounded like a pig giving birth to its babies. The sound woke us like they had some young ones to tend to. This is all I will say. Living in the camp at Vinai, there were many cemeteries. They were mean to us. They didn't let us live in a nice area. Instead they made us live on cemetery land. Hmong are living on the cemeteries with the dead buried just below them.

Hmong are living on the cemeteries with the dead buried just below them.

There is nowhere else to turn. We tried to make the best of it. We were very afraid. One night, Mrs. Chaw, she had an older sister. Mrs. Chaw was sick so she went outside to use the bathroom. While out on the path she overheard two figures by the side of the path in conversation. She thought to herself, "Why? At this time of night? What are they doing out here talking? I wonder who it is?" She was listening and as she listened, the voices were coming from behind the planted sugarcane on the side of the path by the telephone pole. Mrs. Chaw went over to see who it was. She saw a pure white figure running away to the other side. There was nothing there. She was very frightened and scared. She started to walk backward to her shelter. One night later, her older sister passed away. Living in Vinai, it is a scary place. There are many cemeteries and many dead bodies. It was spooky. Our life? We just kept running. We stayed there in Vinai until the children no longer wanted to stay because the Thai kept forcing us to move. That is when we finally came to this country.

Though we are here now, we are still very poor, Auntie. Us. Our life is not like yours at all. We are very poor. Our income has been cut and the children are very depressed about it, Auntie. When we got here, my children didn't know how to register, so our income was cut back. They work outside the home but they are very depressed. We are very poor. We are just simply living in this country. I don't know what else to say. This will be all, Auntie.

What I Have Seen is Very Bad

Mee Lee

I want to tell you about our country and how we lived and did things and about how poor we were. I lived in Laos. I didn't know anything, not even my birth date. I don't even know how we got here or the year. '80? '90? I don't know. My children teach me. I just know a little bit. Like maybe when the Vietnamese were shooting at us. Now I want to tell you more. The teacher has asked me to tell you about us when we lived in our country.

I want to let you know that when we left Laos in 1975, the Vietnamese soldiers were shooting us. We lived in Longcheng in '74, '73, '72, '71. We lived in Bou Long. The Vietnamese soldiers came and we couldn't live there anymore. We moved to Longcheng in 1974. In '75, Vang Pao lost the country to the Vietnamese and he left Laos. We lived there and the Vietnamese tried to kill us, so we went and lived in the jungle. We lived there until the Vietnamese came again in '74, '75. At the time, we lived in the village called Hati, Bou Long. Grandpa Cher Pao, he came back from Thailand and he lived with us again. When General Cher Pao came back, the Vietnamese were shooting at us very much in '74, '75.

There was a lot of shooting in those two years. Then, one night in 1975, they burned our village. They burned our houses. We couldn't stay in the village so we ran to stay in the jungle. The Vietnames burned everything we had. Our houses. Our corn sheds. They took our rice. They killed our chickens, our pigs, and other animals. They made three ways to come and kill us in our village, Hati. One was from Vien Kram. One was from Mount Phou Sa. And one was from Naexai, Non Koung. The Vietnamese made these three ways to come to our village.

Many of our people died. They killed my husband at that time. Our father died and we became very poor. Then, after that, we joined the Chaofa and lived in the mountains and the jungle. In 1976, we came back to Phonsaven and the Vietnamese were very bad to us. They locked us up. They locked the men up. Some of us got away and some were let go. We ran into the jungle and slowly moved through the jungle until we came out in Thailand.

We ran for one year in 1985. Then we got to Thailand in '87. We stayed there the year of '88. In March of 1989, we came to this country. We have lived here three or four years now. We came in March of '89. It has been four years and two months now. Four years and two months since we left and came to this country. Here, we don't hear the sound of knives and guns anymore.

When we ran away, the Vietnamese were shooting at us. That was in '85. We were trying to run away from them. We just stayed in the jungle. We lived in the jungle for five months. We ate wild bushes, fruit, and yams to survive because they burned all our crops and fields and they took all our food. I am very poor. I only had the clothes on my body to take into the jungle. We couldn't take extra clothes to change. We couldn't bring any food or rice to eat at all. They were shooting at us. I just took the children and left. The people who left before us stayed in the cave– they all got killed. Even the ones that they saw running. They all got killed, too. That year, the Vietnamese killed a lot of Hmong and Laotian people who lived in several close villages.

> We lived in the jungle for five months. We ate wild bushes, fruit, and yams to survive because they burned all our crops and fields and they took all our food.

A lot of people died.

I wanted to let you know this because you asked me about it. If you didn't ask, I would not have said anything. I am very poor– that is why I came to this country. If I wasn't poor, I would not be here. If there had not been so much suffering and killing, maybe I would not have come here. Maybe I would not have seen this country at all. I don't know what other people have said, if they had the same problems that I did. I can just tell what I have been through, what I have seen, and what I know of the past. What I have seen was very bad. If General Cher Pao had not come back to live with us, maybe we would not have seen so much killing and suffering in 1974 and '75. Maybe we would not have come to this country.

I want you to know that while we lived for five months in the jungle, every night we slept from one mountain to the next. We ran every day without water to drink, running through the night without any sleep. We stayed in the mountains and we were very afraid that they would come and kill us. We went from one place to another, always afraid, scared all the time. We didn't know where to run next or where to hide. We were very scared, night and day. For five months the Vietnamese shot at us day and night. You could hear the shooting noise all that five months. They shot everywhere: in the mountains, in the street. Everywhere. They were always shooting. They didn't leave at all for the whole five months.

When General Cher Pao came, he told us that we had to get rid of our food and rice. We had to hide it in the jungle and in the caves just in case the Vietnamese would come shooting. When we ran to those places, we could have food and rice to eat when we got there. But when they came and shot at us, we ran away and when we ran, we didn't run to the places where we hid our stuff. We never got that food and rice to eat. They were fighting. For three days and three nights, our people were lost. We just ran. The Vietnamese had more soldiers than we did. They had a lot of guns, knives and ammo. That's why we lost [the war.] We all just ran away with the clothes on our backs. No shoes. Our shoes were all lost during the running.

The soldiers burned everything up. We stuck day and night in the jungles. The mountains. Through every bush, we ran and ran until we got to Thailand. We were very poor. That's why we ran. If nothing happened, we would not have left and come here.

Just know what I have been through and what I have seen. I don't know about other people and how they got here. But, about me, this is what happened. This is why I am here. I don't have a husband. The Vietnamese killed my husband. I just took my three children and followed people anywhere they went until we reached Thailand. This is all there is to let you know.

That is the way I lived in Laos. I'm sure you, as a teacher, have seen from other Hmong families that you have met and from the pictures that people have taken. And that is how our Hmong people lived in Laos. Very poor and sad like that. I don't know your language, so maybe you will have someone translate this so that you can tell what I have said.

So thank you, teacher, and thank all the people who know and teach us everything.

My name is Mee Lee and I thank you very much for listening.

There is Nothing That Will Compare With This Talk

Thao Chong

Thao Chong as Yee Vang stands behind him in their Green Bay home.
Sandra Shackelford Collection, University of Wisconsin-Green Bay, Archives Department.

Yee Vang's husband, Thao Chong, speaks.

I'm very happy to have a person like you to see your smile. You are talkative. Friendly. I like your laughter. Just because I don't speak any English, I am still happy that you came. There is nothing that will compare with this talk. Since I've been here, I tried very much to learn English but I can't say it at all.

I ask Thao Chong his age.

For the real age that my parents gave birth to me would be about 60. When we came to this country, the officials think that I might not be 60, so they put me as 57. Ever since I've been in Green Bay, and I've been all round the city, but there is no one like you. I'm very happy.

Night in a Pig Pen

Yee Vang

Yee Vang in her home in Green Bay, WI.
Sandra Shackelford Collection, University of Wisconsin-Green Bay, Archives Department.

Yee, do you know the year you were born?

I can't remember the year I was born. I don't know. I think, just look at the papers.

How old do you think you are?

I don't know how old I am, but my children calculated and when we got to Phanatnikhom, the official said that I am only 55.

How many children do you have?

I count all of my children including two that have died. I have eight girls and three boys.

How old were you when you had your first child?

I think I was very young. I am not that big yet!

What do you remember of that?

Yes. I can still remember. I am not that big yet! I can remember when I had my first daughter, the one that is speaking here in my tape. (Yee gestures toward her tape recorder.) I think at the time, I was 14, 15-years-old.

What do you remember about having your baby?

I can remember when I had my first child. At the time, I had such a pain in my stomach that I can still remember until now.

Where did you meet your husband?

(*Yee looks at the interpreter and asks if she should talk about "my first husband that I ran away from?"*)

When I got married to my first husband, there is no food to eat. No clothes to wear. Very poor. Very hungry for six months. Just eat a little bit so I don't die. I almost starved. So I ran away to the city called Ta Her. I tossed the ball in the New Year in that city. That is when my husband saw me. After that, I finished my divorce and

I went back to live with my parents. Then my husband came and marry me.

Was it love at first sight, Yee?

After the New Year celebration, we did not see each other at all or talk. After the divorce, he just came and got me.

Was he handsome?

He is not cute. I don't know why I married him!

He is not cute. I don't know why I married him! At the time, he is not cute but he did not have to go to be a soldier in the war. He was still young and chubby. His face was bright. When he got shot by the Vietnamese (Nyab Las), they said that his blood was coming out so much that it soaked one of the blankets. They changed the blanket and threw the other one in the swamp. They said all his clothes are full of blood. So they carried him to a town called Mount Pao Ta Noy. The place was called Pa Pong. They called the airplane to pick him up and take him to the hospital in Sam Thong.

We walked all day past the Nam Ngum River. Some people from up there told us that we should not go because a lot of people up there, the children had diarrhea and died. And even the adults have had diarrhea and died. So you must go back.

So we went back home. We stayed home for one night. The next day we followed the river down. We slept there. The next morning, we reached the big hospital where they took care of those patients. He just got up to wash his clothes.

When I got there, the clothes were full of blood. I told him, "Why can't you wait for me to get here so I can wash it? Why are you in so much hurry to wash this?" (Yee points to her leg just below the knee to show that this was where her husband was shot.) It's from this side all the way through the other side. They used rags and stuffed it in the hole. They asked me to pull it out but I just can't. It made me feel upset inside. That's why he is now skinny and looks like this.

Who was your husband a soldier for?

For the American side. That's when the Americans came and helped with the attack.

Who shot your husband? Was Thao Chang fighting or walking?

They were fighting. The person that shot him was a Green Hmong person but he was with the Vietnamese side. After he got shot, the people behind him saw that he went down. They came and grabbed him and ran. And the other Vietnamese people were following them just like they were following dogs.

How long did it take for your husband to get well in the hospital?

It didn't heal at the hospital. He wasn't there very long. After I got there, my children are still very small. So he told me that he worry about the children and he asked the doctor to let him go. So they did. And we went home. When we got home, he just stayed home and felt the pain until it is all healed up.

I think my husband was in the hospital ten days before I got there. When my husband got shot, there was another man that got shot and died. Some people went to that person's ceremony, but we just went to see my husband. I left my four other little ones at home. At the time, my daughter, Yang, she was still very little. I carried her on my back. When we got half way, I know I shouldn't toss her up on my back, but when I did it, there was a tree branch above our head and it hit the baby's head. She started crying. She cried and cried very much. I was very frustrated. That road is very bad. The worst road that there is. And the edge of the water is so bad. It went up and down. I carried my baby and she was crying. It was so hard for me.

I told my husband that we should go straight home but he wanted to go to Ban Na. So we took the plane to Ban Na. Then we came to Ta Her and then we came home.

Could you have walked home from the hospital?

If he took it very slow, my husband could walk. If we would have walked, it would take a day.

Then what happened?

When we got home, he started healing. We stayed in that town until the war began again. At the time, I had my daughter, Xue. She was ten days old and we started running, running, running until now. We ran to Longcheng Mon Cha. We stayed in Mon Cha. Then I have two sons, Cher and Nao. And then, before we went to Thailand, I had my little baby girl.

When we got there, my husband went to this very big house. There were a lot of people in there. All of my children and I stayed outside in a pig pen for overnight. It smelled so much that we almost didn't last there one night. We were just hiding. They wouldn't let us make a fire or turn on a flashlight. I told my children that we should stay in the mountains but they said it's okay. We should go down and stay with the others. We got down there and there was this little place that had a roof of banana leaves and there had been pigs in there. That's where we spent the night. It so stink. I told my children, "You know how much we've been through? We are suffering from so many things. Our poorness makes us stay in a pig pen." We went to sleep then and the pigs ran out and slept in the woods. We were so scared.

Our poorness makes us stay in a pig pen.

We went to sleep then and the pigs ran out and slept in the woods. We were so scared.

Why didn't you stay in the house?

Because the house has so many people and it just fit their family. And that's why we stayed outside. For people that's so scared, that's why we hide in the pig pen. When we ran up the hill, my son, Nao, was very small. He cried so much I almost threw him away several times because they tried shooting at us. I was holding on to my other son, Cher, Xue and Yang's hand. But my other three kids, they were a little bigger and they can carry stuff on their backs and they can run by themselves. When we ran up the mountain, my oldest daughter said that she wants to hide with my uncle and will run away with them. When we ran up the mountain, there's an orphan boy that is dumb. He cannot talk. His last name is Xiong. He is dumb. He is always running with us. But when we got to the mountain, they stopped shooting. When they shoot, they shoot those big bullets and it sounds like, "naooooo". [Like a scream.] And the people tell me that if my daughter does not catch up to me, she might be running away. So I feel so hurt. I started to cry and I cried so much that I kept blowing my nose. I threw my snot and it hit the dummy who was with us. I was crying and laughing at the same time.

We were so hungry and we got to a field that had so much "*pa la.*" It grows so good. I think it was there to save us. This *pa la* stem is so green. There were crib full of corn in there. We took all the corn and ate them and we clipped up all the "*pa la*" stems and ate them all. When we got the steam, we steamed them and ate them. That's how poor we are. When there's nothing to eat, these are very good.

Why did you decide to run to Thailand?

Why shouldn't I think of going to Thailand? Of course I do think of going because, if we stay, we are so poor and what if they saw us and killed us? We'd rather run. If we don't reach Thailand and if we die halfway, it's better than being killed. Whether we live or die, we are better off running. If we do not do that, maybe we would still be hiding somewhere today.

Yee, tell me about your basket. Did you run with your basket? Did you carry your things in it?

I got that basket in Laos before we came to Thailand. In the woods there is so many rattan trees and that's how people get that to make baskets. When we got to Thailand, I almost threw the basket away. But Kaying said that there's a lot of people that take basket to America. You should take it to America, too, just so you have something to remember it by.

Go back, Yee Vang—when you carried that basket, what was your journey like?

That basket didn't go far. I just carried it from Vientiane across the river to Thailand. The other one that we were running with were all thrown away.

Yee Vang holding her rattan tree basket.
Sandra Shackelford Collection, University of Wisconsin-Green Bay, Archives Department.

How did you cross the Mekong River with all of those children?

Some small rivers we just walked through it. But when we reached the Mekong River, there were some Hmong that saw us and they just told us that they were going across the river, too. So we just went in the boat with them.

We were too scared. If we hadn't met those boys to help us across the river, we might have drowned in the river. I was very scared. Even when we walked through the small river. I carried my basket on my back. I fell down and dropped all the food out of the basket but I was too scared to pick it up. We were starving until we got to Bon Vinai.

Yee Vang and her husband, Thao Chong, holding a photo of her children.
Sandra Shackelford Collection, University of Wisconsin-Green Bay, Archives Department.

A Woman Alone

Pa Thao

Pa Thao stands outside.
Sandra Shackelford Collection, University of Wisconsin-Green Bay, Archives Department.

I am very poor. I had no companion, whether it was to be with me or just to go farming. I was all by myself. Sometimes I would sleep at the garden and with the Spirits out in the forest. I lived that way. I was lucky that my breath of life was not taken away from my body.

I went farming but I could not finish my garden. I did not have enough courage to go and farm by myself. It was a very big forest. There were elephants. I would go out to the farm and run into a patch of elephants in the jungle. I was so scared and frightened. I was too scared, so I spent the night at my garden and came home later. The people farming near me, they told me that they had a lad. He was a Lor. He was an opium addict. He had asked me, "Auntie, please. I am very poor. I don't have any more opium to smoke. Would you allow me to work for you for just one day and you give me several coins to buy myself some opium?"

"Alright. I agree to that," I said. "Why don't you come with me and help me finish the garden? I have a little left that needs to be done. Let's go."

That day he went with me. He helped me the whole afternoon. We took a break, and I asked him to come and join me for a little meal. After eating, he came back with me to the garden. He worked on one end. I worked at the other. He had done a few yards already. I decided to pull some weeds. When I reached down to pull out the weeds, there was a snake sleeping right under the weed by the root. The snake jumped and bit my hand.

The snake jumped up and bit my hand.

"Ahhhhh!" When I looked, blood was gushing from my hand. I told myself to stop and thought, "People said that if you are bitten by a snake, you will die. What am I going to do?" In just a few seconds things became a blur. I swayed back and forth. I could not even call out to the lad to come and kill the snake. I thought, this time I was sure to die. I finally was able to call out to him. When he got to me, I couldn't say any more to him. He searched and looked around for the snake.

While looking, the snake jumped up and tried to bite him, too. He beat the snake to death. Afterwards, he took some snake poop to rub on my hand, but it was still painful. I was in and out [of consciousness]. I felt like I was going to die. The lad helped me back to my shack. Along the way I fell once. I thought, "Well, if I fall once, this is not a very good sign." I knew then that I was not going to get well from the snakebite. I was very scared. I told the lad, "I can't go on anymore. You go and just leave me here. I am either going to get sick or well. When I am doing better, I will come home. Just let me stay here with the spirits."

"Forget it," the lad said. "Just forget it! I will not let you do that. I won't. I came here with you. I will hold on to you until we are home."

When we got home, the younger sister and her husband had just got back from their garden. The lad begged them for help. They did a little black magic on my hand.

That night they also applied some medicine to the wound. My hand was less painful. I slept there the whole night until the morning without moving. They were afraid I was dead. I could not move at all. My arm was as big as my legs are now. I couldn't lift it. Wherever my arm was, it just stayed there.

When I think about it now, I feel angry and heartbroken because I had no husband and no children. When I think of it now, it just breaks my heart. I don't know what else to say. It is no wonder I can't record anything for you because I was this poor. My heart is all broken. I can't even begin to describe how poor I was. I had no younger or older brothers living anywhere. I am this poor.

Life in Laos: Then and Now

Xay Lue Yang

Xay Lue Yang stands in front of a window.
Sandra Shackelford Collection, University of Wisconsin-Green Bay, Archives Department.

I am going to tell about my life back when I was still very young. Back then, when I was young, I didn't know how to support myself. I was poor because our country was in a war crisis. The elders couldn't earn enough to support us. That is why we were so poor when I was very young.

Later, when I was older, I learned how to cook and I could farm. I became more responsible. I was not poor then. I had land to farm. I had livestock: chickens, pigs, cows, and buffaloes. I had almost everything I needed. I was able to support myself. I was well off. I worked hard to support my family. Just about everyone was well off back then, just like every other person in the world. We had money. We were able to provide meals for gathering purposes like everyone else. It was just like every other ordinary day.

I worked hard in my country back then. I knew how to work to support myself. I had farmlands to farm on. I had my own home. I had everything. I had livestock and just about everything. My age then was about 18 to 20 to 30 years old. I knew how to support myself. I was a farmer. Whenever there was no farm work to do, I was free to go out and play. I liked to go out and sell stuff. I liked to wander in the forest and hunt animals.

Our country, Laos, had many kinds of animals. We found our food easily and as often as we wished. We had nothing to worry about. When we looked for food or for work, we didn't need any kind of writing on paper. We had ideas. We had knives and guns to hunt animals. We fed our families and we shared our food with other friends and family members.

There were doe, deer, boar, bear, peacocks in the forest. There were many more animals. There were also wild horses, elephants, rhinos and many, many more kinds of animals living in our country. When we hunted them, we didn't have to purchase any kind of permit to hunt them. We had knives and guns. We hunted as we pleased. We ate as we pleased. We had nothing to worry about. We brought the animals we killed to the family for everyone to eat whether it was a small one or a big one. We called our relatives to come and join us. It was our way of expressing our happiness. There was nothing to worry about. Nothing stressful.

There were also rivers in Laos. Big rivers. There were fishes, all kinds of aquatic creatures in the river. When we wanted to go and play, we found ourselves sticks and went fishing. We did this freely. There was no one to check on us. We didn't need any kind of permit to fish. We just went out and fished. We fished as we pleased. We ate as we pleased. We did everything freely just the way we wanted to.

My life back then? I went out and worked and supported myself. I went fishing. There seemed to be nothing to worry about. How you lived was up to you. You did it like you liked it. There was no one to boss or control you. There was no one to order you around. Everything belonged to everyone. It was owned by the government, but everyone had the right to it.

Finding food to eat was done freely. We fished as we pleased. We netted fish as we pleased. We basketed fish as we pleased. We did everything. Nothing we did broke any laws. We found our source of food freely the way we liked to. We hunted to support our families freely and we ate as we pleased. This is how I lived my life long ago. This is how I supported myself and my family.

It was nothing like being so poor that I had to live in the jungle. There was no such thing back then. Whenever you were free from farming, you took your break and went out and played. You went hunting. Fishing. You trapped fish and netted fish. There were many ways of having fun. Many things you could do freely. We didn't have to pay taxes.

This is what I am going to say. This did really happen. Many people, if you were to ask them, they would say the same thing, too. I have recorded just a couple of things like this into this cassette here and I have talked about how my life was back then in Laos.

We worked and supported ourselves freely in hundreds of ways. We didn't have to pay taxes. We didn't have to purchase any kind of permits to farm. We farmed based on how physically able we were. We didn't break any kind of laws. We worked based on our strengths and how much work we could do. We were strong and had many ideas. It didn't matter how much you hunted. You hunted as much as you wanted. We hunted freely by ourselves. We did it the way we liked it. We did it the way we could do it. Our way of supporting ourselves and our way of hunting animals. We did it the way I have described it.

They say, "Help yourself. Hunt animals." That way you had plenty of food and plenty to feed and plenty to support yourself.

We farmed. It didn't matter how big of an acre it was as long as you had the strength to work on it. The only worry was if you didn't have enough strength to do so. Otherwise, it didn't matter at all. We were not breaking any laws. We could cut down trees. We burned field crops and farmed on the land. Many years ago, the owner of the land, the government, gave us the right to farm for ourselves to make a living from it to support ourselves. We did it freely, the way we pleased. We built our houses. We farmed freely. There was nothing to be depressed about. Nothing was hard for us. This is what I have spoken about. This is how life was back then in Laos. I am going to say this so everyone will know what it was like back then.

We raised our livestock. We sold our livestock. It was easy. We earned money easily. When we raised our farm livestock and we wanted to sell it, we didn't need to get any permits to sell. We sold them freely to whoever wanted them. If we needed it for food, then we just butchered it. We did it freely. We did it the way we liked.

When we were all grown up, we shared everything and passed brotherly and sisterly love within our family. We were farmers. We kept the spirit of love and our physical abilities. There was much love and luck in our land, our country Laos.

But that was a long time ago. Many people and much time have gone by. There was no trouble. No hardship back then. That is the time I have spoken about.

But ever since we were in the war with the Americans, we started living around with no homes. We didn't live in any one steady place. We lived one night in our valley, the next night in another valley. We lived in a house that was not done. Then we moved to the next area.

We lived in places with no permanent farmlands because of the war. That is why we didn't have farms and no permanent home. We moved around to so many places. Eventually we were able to cross over to America. We left behind our brothers, our friends, our relatives, our sisters and many, many more. The ones that could not come here, they stayed behind. The ones that didn't want to stay behind, stayed behind anyway. They were not able to contact anyone or they just didn't know how to come because they were simple farmers. They didn't know how to lead the way so they had to stay behind. They moved from jungle to jungle, living in the jungle and everywhere. They were poor. They lived like animals. Like a deer. They lived and ate like a wild boar or bear. They ate vines. They ate the heart of bamboo trees. They ate weeds, too.

They were poor.

They could not come.

They didn't make it.

They were shot.

Now they are dead.

There are many I could talk about, but I am not sure of them any more. I do know that I had a brother and some sisters that were left back in Laos. They can't come here anymore. My brother? He is still alive. This particular brother, he was in the war. He was captured and taken prisoner, but he is still alive.

My sister and brother-in-law? My sister moved. She didn't want to live in Laos anymore. She couldn't stand being so poor. She couldn't stand the life of being married to a husband involved with war. That is why she moved and wanted to come to America. She moved around everywhere.

But she didn't make it.

She died of starvation.

Some people were shot. Some died of starvation. Some died of illness. My sister and brother-in-law both died. Almost all of their children died, too. Their sons. They had three sons. Two are dead. Only one is left. They had two daughters. The two daughters and both their parents died. Only the youngest son survived. He was brought up by one of the younger brothers [relatives]. Right now, he is living very poorly. He has no parents. No relatives. No brothers. He has no idea what to do to support himself. He has no role model. There is no one to teach him. There is no one to show him how to take care of himself. He is very poor.

There is also one of my uncle's daughters left behind in Laos. One of his daughters is in the same situation. She lost one son and her father. There was also one sister left and three sons. That sister, she died, too. Now, there are three sons left back in Laos. They are very poor though. There is no one to teach them. They have no beds in the place where they sleep. Their pots and pans, their mats. They live just like some orphans. The reason? The war. Every year they cry about not having relatives and not having parents and being so poor and not having someone to love them. They cry because they have no one to help them. Once or twice a year, they write me and beg us to come and visit, to come and help them. But we don't have the money. They ask us for money to help them build their family. They have cried and begged for help many times. We think of them. We miss and love them very much. But we are poor, too. We have nothing to give them that would help them or show them how much we love them. The more I think of them, the more it breaks my heart.

I finally made a decision. I thought, maybe I should visit them once to see if my brother is still living or just to see how he is living. If he is still in the same condition as before or just to see why he cries so much. I made up my mind to go and visit our country and to see the country once more, to see how it is like now. I made my decision to go back and visit Laos and to go and see the place where my mom and dad gave birth to me.

You missed your old home. Your old farmland. Your rice field. Your country. Everything. Though you didn't wish to cry, tears just came to your eyes anyway.

Though you didn't wish to cry, tears just came to your eyes anyway.

We went back to our country and saw the places. We saw the river where we used to drink from. We saw the trees and the bamboo.

We saw the fields we used to work. We went back and saw some of the people that we used to live with. Happiness! We were happy indeed! We were as happy as when our mothers gave birth to us. We were very happy just to step on the ground again. To drink the water there again. To go and eat rice there. We were very happy. We saw the children. Everyone. The brothers. Our hearts went out to them, and we loved them dearly. But when we came to this country — to America — we couldn't work to earn any kind of money to help them at all.

When they came and saw us, it was as if we were looking at starving children. They cried very much. Everyone cried. All we could do was pat their heads. We loved them but there was nothing we could do. We saw how poor they were. I am telling this as a historical moment. It was very poor. Three of them has been separated from their parents. Their father had left them, then their mother had left them, too. Toukee was separated from his mom and dad, and his mom and dad were separated from Toukee. He was very poor. His house was like a shack. When we were outside, you saw through to the inside. When you were inside, you saw through to the outside.

Why does it have to be this way? The reason is because of the war. Don't they have what it takes to build a decent home or is it because they don't have the money to do so? If this is the case, they are very poor and our hearts go out to them. But we have no money to send to them, no way to help them at all.

Today, I have recorded the world like this to preserve for the grandchildren or other parents like us to listen to and to hear about our people; about how poor they are, how depressed they are; about the life of orphans. The life of people who don't have parents or relatives; about people who have no friends. All these are dying, too, because we have separated from each other. One has left another and everyone misses each other very much. This is how it is. Everyone, if you listen to this, please pardon and excuse me. For those of you who are more well off, please love the people who are orphans and who are poor. This is all I have to say. I have only spoken just a little bit about my country and returning to visit it and the people. I was not going to say a lot.

This is what I have to say to everyone.

A Life

Sao Soua Ly

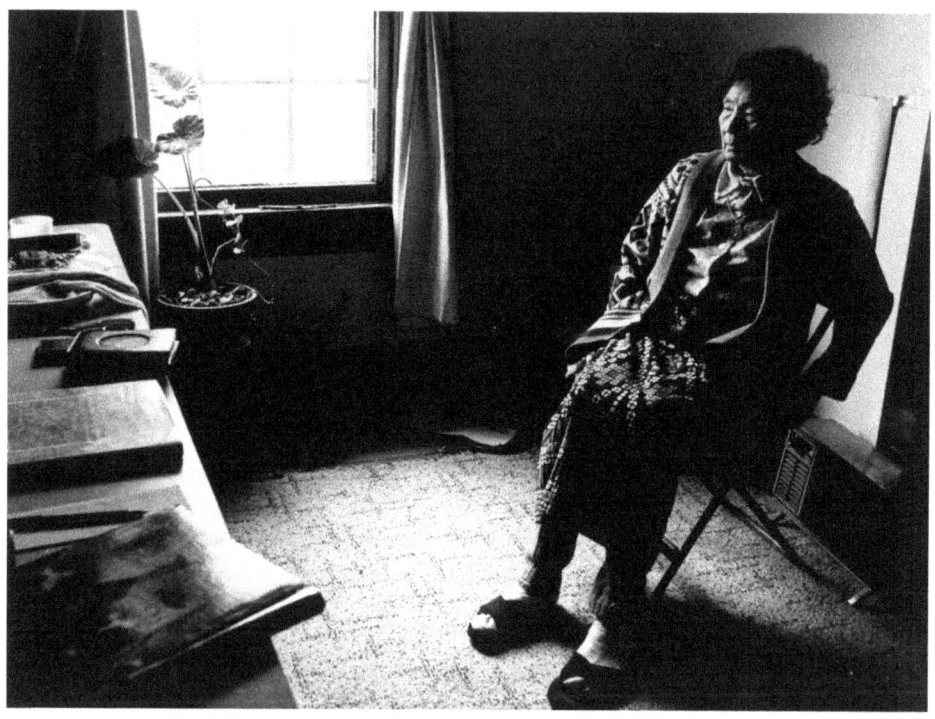

Sao Soua Ly in her home.
Sandra Shackelford Collection, University of Wisconsin-Green Bay, Archives Department.

Today it's a happy day. Sandy and May Neng have come to talk to me. I am Sao Ly. Americans called me Sao Soua Ly. But Hmong called me Soua Ly. Today is April 22, 1991. I am happy that I am an elderly person. I am 67.

Speaking from my voice, I sound young and I am still pretty strong, but–they said–not old. If people heard my voice, they would say I am still young. But if you saw me, I am old! But this teacher, Sandy, she saw me and she loved me very much. She came to see me. She will teach me one hundred things, and I will tell her about my life in this cassette so she can write a story on it for me to keep it. So, if there are relatives or friends who would like to learn more about my story, I could have them look at it and see if they would love my life.

Soua, where were you born?

I was born very far away in Vietnamese country, a town called Chua Cher near Nong Het and Xiengkhouang Province.

Were you born in 1924?

Oh, 1918. I don't know how old I was but I asked this from my brother and my son, and they want me to go to the church and talk about my life. They just tell me that I am 67 years old but maybe now it's more.

73 years old?

They gave it to me from my Social Security card but now I don't know anything. So now I am 73 years old.

Tell me about your village: what it looked like, the house you remember.

Yes. I still remember my house at Chua Cher. My father and mother built it very big. We used wood walls and a wood roof.

Your mother and father... what were their names?

My mother's name was Lue. My father's name was Wa Houa Ly. My mother's last name is Lor. Lue Lor.

How many children did they have?

They have four children.

What were their names and what is your position in the family?

The oldest one is called Xai. I am the second one, Soua. And the one next to me is called Pa, and the youngest boy is called Txhis.

Were you the prettiest?

Yes, I am the prettiest, but my younger sister is almost as pretty as me!

Yes, I am the prettiest, but my younger sister is almost as pretty as me! My older sister is not as pretty as us but she is a very hard-working person and people like her. People wanted to marry her, and they also wanted to marry me.

How did your mother and father make a living?

About my father, I don't know and I don't remember because he died when I was very small. I do not remember how old I was when my father died. Maybe ten. I don't know. My brother was very little. At that time, he didn't know how to sit yet. After my father died, my mother got married again. Then we didn't have a mother and a father. We just stay with my father's brother. We farmed for food and crops. But my uncle is a salesman. He sells fabrics to make money.

What did he sell?

He was a salesman. With materials and crops. All I know is that when he came back, he brought money back.

What kind of little girl were you? Did you play games? Tell me about your childhood.

I don't remember that I played with my brother and sisters. We had farm animals and we just had to watch over the animals. Daylight came and we watched over the animals until dark until you got to be a woman, and then you worked in the crop fields.

How did you take care of the animals? What kind of animals were they? Did you give them names?

We do have names for them. We took care of cows, horses and buffalo. So when the sundown came, you called them to come home.

"Ha Haaaa!" [calling the horses to come home.] The buffalo. I can only remember I named Bucktow. "Bucktow! Tell the others to come and we'll go home." So that one comes first followed by the others. Then you climbed up on that one and he lead and the others follow.

Did you like being out in the field? Was it pretty? What was it like?

Being out there was very scary. (Cries.) The countryside was very scary. We don't have a mom and dad. They told us to go, so we had to go.

It was not fun? It was frightening? Why were you scared?

Because it's all bushes and banana tree fields. I was afraid of tigers because at that time there were a lot of tigers and there was the curse. The curse rides on the back of the tiger. Tiger bite.

Please explain this curse.

I never saw it before, but people kept saying that curses ride on the tiger. When you are a kid, they tell you that. You get very scared. After that, I got to be a young lady and that's when I started farming and I didn't have to watch over the animals. When we did farming, we cut down trees and bushes, and started planting the crops.

You learned about farming. Did you also learn about reading and writing?

In my country, they don't let the girls learn to read and write.In my country, they don't let the girls learn to read and write. They just let the boys learn how to read and write. All the girls had to learn was how to do the harvesting and then get married.

How do you feel about that?

I don't feel anything about it. In my country, the boys had to be educated and the girls did not have to be educated. All you think about is making beautiful *paj ntaus* to wear.

Sao Soua Ly sewing.
Sandra Shackelford Collection, University of Wisconsin-Green Bay, Archives Department.

Where did you meet your husband?

At first, I turned 16 and I was very beautiful. Hmong [people] saw me and they pulled with me to get me to their houses to get me married. At the time, I was very pretty and a very hard-working lady, and my uncle loved us very much so people liked me very much. But our Hmong people, when you go to the farm field, they try to capture you on the way.

The first man, I didn't know him and I didn't like him. Our Hmong people, if they want to marry you then they take things from you. They take your clothes and they threw one of their things to you. And when the parent comes and the people said that they got my things and that they wanted to marry me. But for some parents, if they don't like that man or those people, then they won't let you marry them either. And you must have one witness. If your parent asks you if you really gave your things to the people, the witness must say, "No, she didn't. They just throw her their stuff and they tear some from her clothes." Then your parents say, "Okay. She didn't give it to you so you must let her go. If you don't let her go, I will fight you! Because we love our daughter very much. If she doesn't like you and she goes with you, she will cry."

So after that, my husband came along but I never knew him. We never talked. He came and married me. So I saw him and I think I like him, too. And this is why I married him. He heard people talk about me and he just came.

How old were you when you went with him?

18 years old. But when you turn 16, you are very beautiful and you work very hard and the family and my people like you very much. They look for a hard-working person.

What did your husband look like?

Oh, my husband is small, slim, but he is very handsome. When he laughs, his teeth are so white. We don't have any pictures left of him. Now, I don't have a son or daughter that looks like him except one daughter in California that looks like him.

No, they didn't look like me. They looked like the father but not as beautiful as their father.

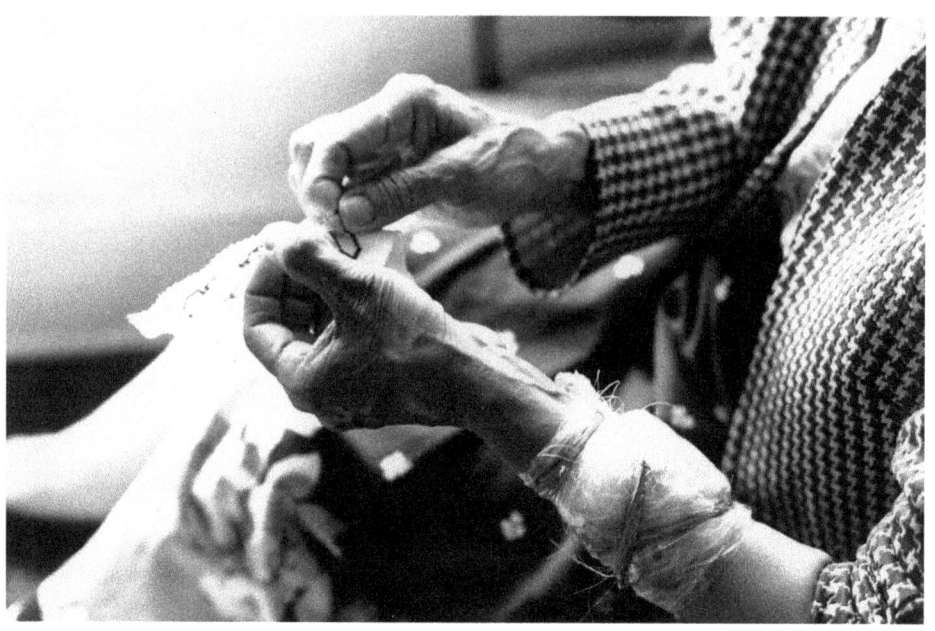

A close-up of Sao Soua Ly sewing.
Sandra Shackelford Collection, University of Wisconsin-Green Bay, Archives Department.

What was your marriage like? Did you live on a farm?

Oh. I got married to my husband very far away from my house because I lived in the town that has wars. The town was called Nong Het. Because in the town of Nong Het, many brothers and relatives became fighters.

At the time, there were French and Vietnamese. My husband was not a fighter. They [his family] were not warlike people, but they lived in a Vietnamese town. We were very poor. We had been married 20 days and the Hmong Vietnamese came and captured me and my husband and took us to a town called Muang Seng.

Why did they arrest you?

Because they said I was a Ly clan girl. And the Ly clan was the first clan that helped the French in the war. I was given free to my husband and so the Vietnamese thought that my husband might be a traitor. He would make a way for the French to go and shoot them. That's why they captured us.

How was it in the village?

When they captured us, they took all my silver. I had many silver bracelets on. Two bracelets makes one silver piece and I had four big ones on my arms. They took it all. And I had some stuff in my luggage. They asked my family which luggage is the daughter-in-law's luggage. They took all my clothes and silver. After they took that, they pointed guns at us and took us away. They took us to stay with the Hmong Vietnamese leader called Fai Dang Lor. And they took one of my husband's brothers with us. They didn't do anything bad to us, they just made us stay in the house.

We cooked for ourselves in their house. We stayed there until one Hmong Vietnamese leader, who lived in a town called Keng and was my husband's father's leader, he came and rescued us.

He said to the Vietnamese leader in Muang Seng, "It is not that they gave her free to her husband. Her husband's family paid 20 silver bars for her." And he said, "The Hmong Lor clan, before she was young, they saw her. We think they just wanted to take our daughter-in-law away. We bought her off. We paid too much money for her. We should not believe these Hmong Vietnamese people. So we'll just take our daughter and son away."

That took much courage to go and rescue you, didn't it?

He was like a general to the Hmong people. He did have a lot of courage to rescue us.

Did you go with him? Where did you go?

So we came with him and we went back and stayed with my mother and father-in-law for three months. Then they came back and captured us [again].

Then where did they take you?

When they came, people heard about it. They told us that we were going to be captured by the Vietnamese. So they came and told us that, they said, "Tonight they are going to capture you." So that night, our family all ran away. We left our chickens and pigs and our house. We ran and ran for five days until we got to Muang Nham.

Did you run on a road? How far did you travel? Did you go by foot? What was it like to run for five days?

We ran on the road.

Long ago, when we ran like that, we went up the hills and down the hills. Up the hills and down the hills. Very crooked. Very hungry. Our legs felt like they were going to fall apart. Each of us cried on our own. By saying this, it makes me very sad.

My husband's family was very, very upset with me because they said it was because of marrying [that] girl. Because of marrying [that] girl, that was why the Vietnamese tried to capture her and that made us very poor, running with her. If we don't run with her, maybe they will kill us. And if we would give our daughter-in-law away, we don't feel that we could give her away either. But if we don't give her to them, they would kill us. That's why we have to run. It didn't matter how much they got upset with me, they had to run with me anyway.

How did you feel about that?

I think they blamed me. At the time I think that my parents did not join in the war, but friends and relatives were joining with the French. So that's why they blamed me. And they just wanted to make trouble for me. If I knew that this was going to happen, I would never have married.

What city did you live in?

They called it Muang Nham and Muang Moc. Americans said Muang More but Hmong said Muang Nya.

What did you do in that city? How did you live?

We settled there and the land was good for raising crops. All the people in the village were very kind to us. They welcomed us. They gave us land to plant crops. They gave us seeds and they got food for us to eat.

Is this where your children were born?

Yes.

How many?

In this town I had three children.

Was it a peaceful town?

At first it was good and peaceful. We were there for two years. The third year the French arrived and there was a big war, and then we ran again. This time it was even harder than the last time. We were even poorer than the last time.

Where did you run?

We lived in Muang Nham and my brother-in-law went to be a soldier. Two brothers were soldiers with the French. So the French fought the Vietnamese. After that they brought my brother-in-law back.

For three days after, the Vietnamese arrived in Muang Nham and they came to capture my husband, my two brothers-in-law, and me. Then we sent the brother that worked with the French to Xieng. After that we stayed for one year in Muang Nham and then the Vietnamese kept trying to capture me and my husband, but we got away before they got us.

By saying this, it is very sad. So at night, people heard about it and they let us know we were going to be captured by the Vietnamese. So that night we ran away from the house. Just left the kids and the older people in the house. So morning came and they said maybe we don't have to be scared anymore. So I came back home to feed the pigs and all of a sudden, I was just chopping the pig food, and I looked around and the Vietnamese were standing all over. And I said, "Oh God! Now what are we going to do?"

So one of my older brother's-in-law came out and said, "Sister Koua. Are you going to go?" Then I put my baby on my back. And I took one pail so it would look like I was going to get water. They were looking, too. But right after those bushes was the way to brothers-in-law and my husband's hiding place. If I go there, they will spot me. So there's a path behind those bushes. I took my baby. I carry it on my chest and I crawl down the path. I started crawling when the sun was coming up and when the sun was half sideways down because I don't have a watch. That's when I got to my brother-in-law and my husband's hiding place.

When I got there, they put some leaves over the hiding place door. I said to myself, "Oh God! Maybe they ran away." They had an ax and maybe they ran away to Xieng. Then I called out. I said, "Choia Koua! Are you still here or are you gone?" And they whispered from down the path, "Come down here. We are down here."

When I got there, I told them that the Vietnamese had come to get us. "I have been running all day today until I got here. But my brother-in-law, Nao, they are still butchering pigs to eat. They are giving our names to our brothers-in-law." And my husband said, "You stay here and we will go peek and see what they are doing."

At that time, they [the husband and brother-in-law] had guns and hand grenades. So I stayed. They went and saw that right after they ate, the Vietnamese captured my two older brothers-in-law. They used rope to tie them up. So they took them away and my husband came back to get me. We went back to the house and he said, "From now on, being husband and wife, we must see each other just now. We have to run away. You women stay and if they come and take you, you do whatever they say. Okay? If they want you to be their wife, do what they say so they don't kill you. Whatever happens to me doesn't matter." My sister-in-law and I started crying. We cried so much.

What happened to them?

After that, they took their guns and things and went away. One night, they saw a Vietnamese soldier take my brother-in-law to a small town. They ran to try and get ahead and wait for them. They went to the next small town and told the leader to have somebody go and tell the Vietnamese soldiers that we were waiting for them and that we are going to kill them if they don't let go of my brothers. If they don't let go, we will shoot right now. And the messenger told them the message. And the Vietnamese soldier said, "We are not afraid of them! They have only two guys and we have five. Don't be afraid," he said.

But they also had captured thirty other prisoners with my two brothers-in-law. And they took so many of them that the messenger guy said, "If you don't stop and you keep going, they are really going to shoot you." And the Vietnamese soldier said, "No. No. No. Don't be afraid."

Then my husband and my brother-in-law ran through a little village where they were still celebrating New Years. They ran a little ways past that town and then they stayed way up on top of the hills. When the Vietnamese soldiers and the other prisoners came down the path past the town, they started shooting right at them.

They fired just like bombing from the airplane. Then all the prisoners all lay down in the path and the two Vietnamese were killed and the other three said, "Don't be afraid. They are not going to shoot us." And my two brothers-in-law and the others started running. They kept running and taking their ropes off. They ran and ran until they got back home. My husband had killed two Vietnamese soldiers. The other three got away.

And then what happened?

When we got home, we all cried but at the time there was no soldiers anywhere to help us. All the soldiers and the French had gone back home. All my husband and brother-in-law had were one gun and hand grenades. So we butchered all the pigs and chickens to eat. After we ate, we ran to stay in the jungle for one month. Just the four of us: my brother-in-law, my sister-in-law and our children. My two older brothers-in-law that they had captured with my parents and the four of us ran for three days and three nights until we got to San Tong.

They called it Thathom Thaviang because the French are still there, that's why we went there. For three months we asked the French to go back there but they couldn't get through. And then my husband and brother-in-law went back and they couldn't make it so they came back. They came back and we stayed there for a while. We lived in the jungle outside of the village. There was no food to eat. We just bought it from the Laotians very far from the village where they lived. We just ate vegetables and vegetables.

Then one day, my husband and brother-in-law went back and tried to rescue my parents-in-law and my children. They brought them back and we started running for eight days. And we hadn't reached Xieng. We just got to Muang Ong. And we settled there. We served as soldiers in that town for three years. Then the war stopped. Then we stayed there for a long while. Then we moved to Xieng.

Then the War, Kong Lai [French Indochina War] started. And that's the time my husband went to war and passed away. So did my brother-in-law. They all died. And then we lived in Phou Khoun with no husband.

So after that, we just ran with the General Vang Pao. They sent us to many places and we settled in Longcheng. We stayed there until General Vang Pao ran away to America. We followed him. Then I think that because this is the Vietnamese War, too, and if we stayed, maybe the Vietnamese would know that my husband was a soldier and they would kill my children. And I think my children will be tortured, too. So that's why we ran again. That's why we got very afraid and started running again.

Was your husband a soldier for the French?

Yes. They were killed by the Vietnamese. It's a jungle out there and I don't know where they were killed. All I know is that they were killed. They never found his body.

When you were running, was most of the fighting between themselves, the French and Vietnamese? Did you see any Americans?

After the French War, Americans began just as we were leaving the country.

All of the fighting you saw was between the French and the Vietnamese then?

Yes.

Soua, tell me about your journey to freedom.

Before we came to this country, we lived in Longcheng. Then we said we were going to harvest in Vientiane. And then we harvest there for a while and we heard gossip that if you had a son and if your husband was a soldier, you couldn't stay. If you stayed, you would be tortured. At that time, all my daughters were married and all I had was my son with me. My son and I crossed the Mekong River to Thailand and we stayed there until my brother in Colorado sponsored us to this country.

You left Longcheng. How long did the journey take? Were you frightened?

From Longcheng to Vientiane, we traveled by taxi. It took one day to get there. But at the time, we didn't bring anything. We just took one change of clothes for each of us. One shirt and one pants. That was 1975.

We crossed the Mekong River by boat. We paid 20,000 kip for both me and my son. At the time, it was still cheap.

How much would that be in American money?

I think they said $100 was 2,000 kip. But I am not sure. Maybe it's more like 20,000. But now they use Vietnamese money instead of Laos money.

But it was all you had.

I was poor at the time. Just enough to pay for the boat fare and a little left over for food.

How old was your son?

At the time, my son was 20 years old.

Were you frightened?

No. We were not scared because at the time there were many people going with us. But all the others were woman and maybe they were a little smarter than us because when we got off the boat, they ran right away.

My son thought he would let the women go first. After they got out, this Laotian man almost cheated us. He told us to pay him more money. But at the time, I think I was smart, too! So my son said, "We have already paid to the owner across the river and there is no way we can pay you more." He said, "You must pay." My son said, "You don't feel that it's fair?"

And the boatman said, "No. You must pay more."

And then my son said, "If you think it's fair than you take me back to the owner across the river and I can tell him to give you the money."

And then I said, "No! No way!! He just lied to you. Don't go back there with him, Are you scared?"

And my son said, "No. I am not scared." My son said to the boatman, "If I go, will you take me back?"

I held my son's arm. I would not let him go. And I said to the boatman, I said, "Why didn't you tell the others, too? You just tell me and my son. Do you know that my husband is in Heaven? We already paid to the other man across the river. Are you trying to cheat us? Why didn't you ask the others to pay more, too. Do you know my husband is in heaven? Aren't you afraid that he will break your neck if you cheat us? Aren't you scared to die?

"No, my son. Don't go with him. He just lied to you because he already got paid. Why do you believe him?" And then I pulled my son's arm three times and we just ran and the boatman just rode off and I told my son, "See, my son! I said some old people don't respect. See! I was right!!"

Soua, what was the most frightening thing that happened to you on this journey?

What's the most scaring time that makes me afraid? The time that my husband told me that if we ran away and they captured us, we were going to be their wife. At the time, you knew you were still alive but it seemed like your heart is beating and you had no body. That's when I got very scared.

Once you got across the Mekong River, what did you do?

We caught up with the others and we walked up to the street. The car that picked up people from the river took us to the camp. We each paid 200. That was to Camp Nong Khai.

What was the camp like?

We stayed for 10 days in that camp. The American Embassy gave us rice and food and helped us with shelter.

What were the conditions like in that camp?

When we came, there wasn't many people and it wasn't like a camp. They just took us to stay in the Buddhist Temple. After 10 days, they took us to Camp Nam Phong.

When did you come to the United States?

Hmmm. I forget what year. I think it was '78.

How was your airplane trip? What did you bring with you to the United States?

When we came to this country, we didn't bring anything because we didn't have anything. We lived in Thailand very long and we got very poor. We had just enough to eat. Just enough to live.

Out of that poverty, taking you away from everything you knew and coming to a country you couldn't imagine, what was your heart doing?

When I came and I first got interviewed in this country, I already had dreams about seeing this country. I thought when I got here, it would be the same as in my dream. All my relatives and all the people that were closest to me left and came to America so I decided to come, too. And all my daughters, brothers, sisters-in-law, aunt and sisters were in the United States. So I was very happy to come but still I miss the land of my country.

Soua, what was your airplane like?

I didn't see anything. They put me in a window seat, too. There were all clouds outside and I didn't see anything and I thought, "Where am I going? Where am I going to be? Am I really going to see my people or not? Is it really true?" I was seasick, too.

When you stepped off the airplane, how did you feel?

We arrived in California. And then we missed our other plane so we stayed there overnight. I thought, "Where are we"

Where are we going to be?" But at that time, my son speaks English, too. A little bit, like me now. But the people told us we would depart, but we waited until 10 o'clock.

But we hear one of the American ladies that flies with us. She told my son that, "She brother called me. She hungry." (*Soua's brother had called the airport and told them his mother's brother called the airport and told them his mother might be hungry.*) "My son said, "Uncle called them and told them to find us some food. Maybe we are hungry." And we go with her [the American lady.]

And I was so dumb. Very dumb. I didn't know what kind I should eat! I just took two pieces of bread that had nothing in there but lettuce. And we didn't know what to drink. They just gave us a glass of cold water. And after they fed us, she said, "Is that enough? If it is not enough, go get some more." I don't know why I was so shy. I told her it was enough. Because Hmong is so shy.

With all of these things that happened to you in your life, do you feel any anger in your heart?

I was sad and felt very stressed that I was poor. But I didn't think of that. I just thought, "I still have my life and my eyes to see my family., my friends, my relatives." So I didn't think of being depressed. Because if you think of it, you still have that grief inside of you. Even the king has grief and he doesn't think about it, too.

Soua, do you have a wish for this world?

Well, right now this heart does not know what to think or what to say to anyone. It looks like you try to say a good word to them to get them to say a good word back, for you to feel good and know how to think and have friends and know how to love each other even though you visit each other. Just make one phone call and talk to each other and that makes me very happy. But I think that I am old so nobody loves me. And that's one grief that is always in my heart.

According to me, when I got to this country, I had lived with my brothers and I never got depressed. I was not poor. I was not rich. I was okay. Even when you are small, even though it's not your

real parents, you just get poor when you are little. But ever since I grew up, they (Soua's aunts and uncles) always loved me.
Because my uncle and my brother are all working and we are not poor. But ever since I got my daughter-in-law, then we didn't divorce her or separate with her but she ran away.

I have a lot of grief in my heart. She did so many bad things to me. I didn't know that she was always that way and that she only married for a few days and then she wanted to be single again. Because I don't know how her heart thinks.

She always said that she wanted to be a good person. She was always away. I wonder why because I already married her to my son. She always said that but she does what her heart tells her to do. She ran away but she didn't divorce my son either. She is just gone and gone. She married for a few days and came back. I didn't know what to do. Right now, I carry this grief in myself for the past three years and it makes me crazy. Sometimes I put things somewhere and I can't remember where I put them. It's like you can't even remember your own people.

If I pray to God to love me, would He love me?

If I pray to God to love me, would He love me? And if I prayed to God to keep me from sickness and having so much grief and let me live until the day I die so I could stay with God, will I be living happy or will I be poor like this? I always think, to be good and to have good things. But maybe God is with me and He is poor with me that I didn't know about. But will He love me? Because now I believe in God.

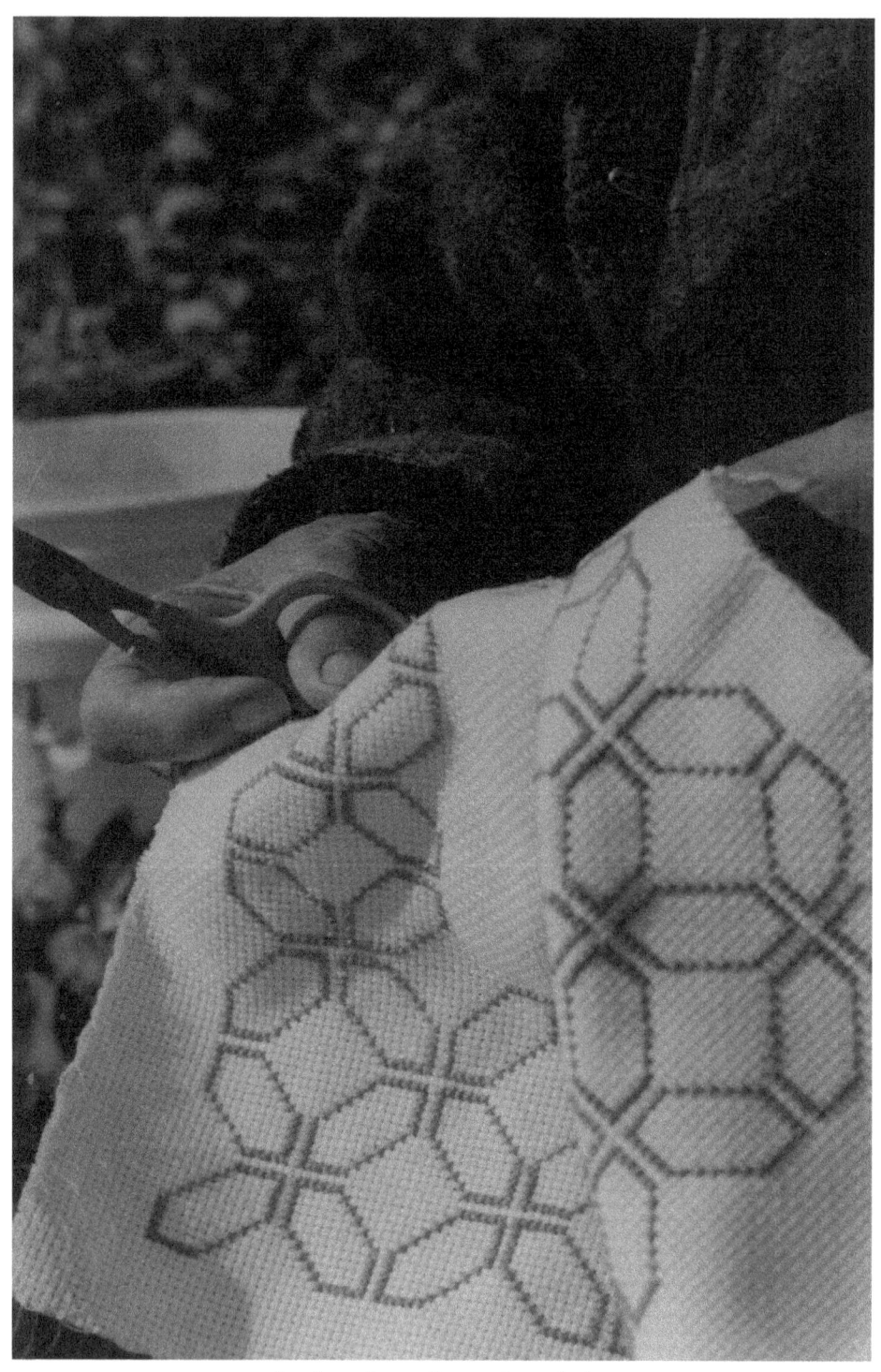

Sao Soua Ly cutting a story cloth.
Sandra Shackelford Collection, University of Wisconsin-Green Bay, Archives Department.

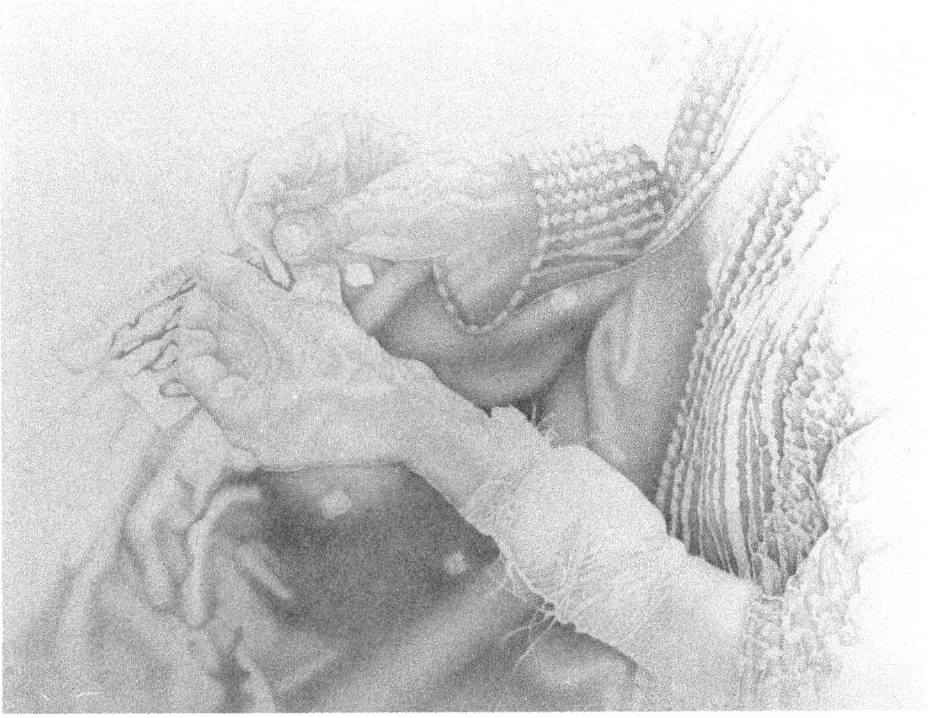

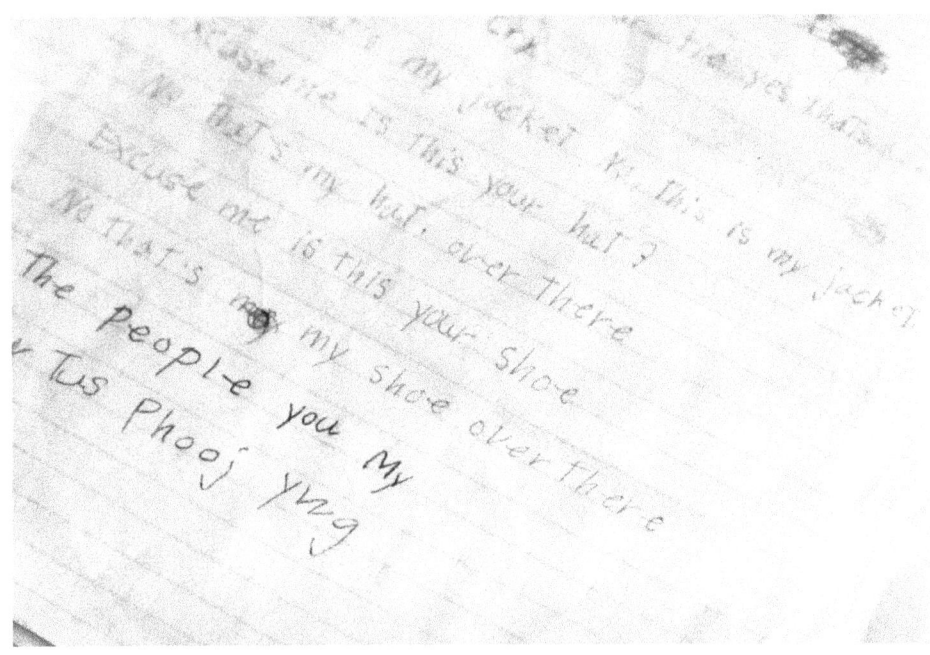

Sandra's drawing of Sao Soua Ly's beautifully aged hands.
Sandra Shackelford Collection, University of Wisconsin-Green Bay, Archives Department.

Sao Soua Ly's English handwriting.
Sandra Shackelford Collection, University of Wisconsin-Green Bay, Archives Department.

I Will Tell What I Know

Nor Chia Lor

Nor Chia Lor in his kitchen.
Sandra Shackelford Collection, University of Wisconsin-Green Bay, Archives Department.

Here I am. I'm Nor Chia or Nhia Koua Lor. On this cassette I will tell you about life in the past and about things that our great grandparents always have done. I will tell about that in this cassette. About the old ways that the elderly who took us from China, [because I haven't been there] I just heard them talk and tell about us [the Hmong people] moving to Laos. I will talk about what I know since moving to Laos.

The story of the past in China would have to be told by the great grandparents. I will talk about what I have seen. And about my life until today.

We have parents and friends but at first when we come and live in Laos and have a house and property, we are also the people who are responsible for the community I have lived in. Of course, our grandfathers, Kia Tong Lo, Fai Da, and Nhia Fu, they are the elders who look after us and the community.

Our country was breaking apart because of people wanting to become powerful in politics. Whoever became governor or senator when the French overcame us. If one person became mayor or governor or senator, everyone [the little people like us] had to obey. We had to respect those officials. If the French needed something, that mayor in your town must get it for them. If they need tax money, the mayor must take everyone's pay. That person that is the boss is the person that works for the French. He is the messenger between the French and the community. Because people at the time do not know about what the government is doing [politics]. They have to do what they are told.

Grandpa, Grandma, Mom, and Dad — they always worked. They did not have time to stay home and rest because each year they had to pay taxes to the French. Taxes are not little; they are a lot. Each head of household had to pay seven kip [as big as a silver dollar though worth more] for every gun in the house. If you had a cow, you pay seven kip also. Only the buffalo you did not have to pay taxes for.

Each person is seven kee. Hmong people, we work hard digging from the ground to feed us. If you have to pay 30 or 40 kip each year, how are we going to feed ourselves? Our people cannot pay these taxes. That's why people want to be politicians. So they will not have to pay taxes. Ever since I knew my grandpa, Kia Tong, he was the mayor. That's how my parents and our grandparents got jobs. In our country, if there was someone who was educated and became a leader and treated everybody equally, then maybe our lives would not have been so dark.

In our country, if there was someone who was educated and became a leader and treated everybody equally, then maybe our lives would not have been so dark.

There are a lot of people who want to be mayor or senator because that's all they do — relay messages between the people and those in power. That's the people and those in power. That's his job.

The people do not see [have] the freedom or the power to do what they want. And they don't know if they have the right to change things because there is no school. There is no education. That's why everyone is naive and they can't read and write for four to five generations. Because there's nobody who is educated to teach those people.

Hmong people live in big communities but there is no school, no hospital to help educate them. That's why we never see or know about freedom and how to tell what is good or bad; how to earn money to support our families. That's why we are digging in the ground as farmers to feed ourselves.

When the French were collecting taxes, those people who had jobs to pay taxes could live well. People who were poor and were orphans, whose parents died and left them, they don't have the money for insurance and taxes for the price of food and livestock. Those people moved to Vietnam. Why they moved to Vietnam is because the Vietnamese have big forests. It's far and nobody could come because the forests are very big. You could go ten or more days and there is no way out of there. That's why everybody moved into that forest.

[We] go there, not because we like to stay there or want to hide from something. We just want to get away from paying taxes because the taxes are very high. That's why some of our people moved right into Vietnam's property and some of them moved just to the border. In our country, there's not one street. Just a big jungle.

In that country, there's not one street. Just a big jungle.

The people had moved from work to live in Vietnam. They didn't take Vietnam's side or the Lao side. They run to be jungle people. In Vietnam, the capital is called Moua Long. Moua Long has two or three places that's called the same thing. There's one in Laos. But the place that we all run to is Vietnam, that's the capital, Moua Long. Pa Ker, Ka Chua Pli, La Tsa Tsoo, Ti Uwa, and Pa So, and Why Na Me. And we moved to these properties because we are leaving our work. [My grandmother, my grandfather and my parents [inaudible.] At the time, I was only a month old. I had run to live in Vietnam until I grow big. Like they said, I could go to the farm by myself then I came back to the country [Laos], Nong Het, the country that is ruled by the French.

When I got in there, I was not lucky. My mother died and left me. Then my father got remarried and left me with my sisters, my brothers. We all were still very young. We cannot plant crops. We cannot farm.

In this country, making a farm, you have to make a fence around it otherwise the cows and the buffalo will eat it all. We cannot make a big fence and eat. Because of the work then is hard. That's why I became a soldier.

The reason that I became a soldier is because we cannot pay taxes. The table named before that, the Hmong Lor takes care of that. I had said my grandfather, Kia Tong was the one that takes care of that. Our country was the Hmong Lee that were the people who takes care and had power to it… Which means: the family business before that, my grandfather owned. Now the country is being taken care of by the Hmong Lee Clan because they had more power and education. Their children are more educated.

[They] have cows and money. They let their sons go play with girls, go ride houses, go bull fighting, and gambling. That came from the Hmong Lor Clan because they don't know how to lead.

Chong Tou is one of the mayors of Laos when the French took over and when we came from China. He's the first person to become mayor. And he is Mayor Chong Tou. After that then, the Hmong Lee came and married… [inaudible] because they didn't get to become powerful political people. That's why they came and married our [Lor] sisters, our cousins and aunts to be their wives. To be wives, to have children. That's when they have Pin Ya Bee Le Fong, Grandpa Lia, Grandpa Ger. [They are all Le Fong's children.]

Then, they let all these kids [the Lees] go to school. The Lees let them go to school in Laos and when they get to the third grade, they send them to school in France. That's when the French came and took over our country. Six or seven years and then came back. The kids speak French. Whatever they say is right because the French took over the country. Because they speak French, what was wrong they said was right, or they made it right. And if you lose, they made you win. No matter what happened, if they [the kids who speak French] tell them they win, then they will win.

When they [the Lors and the Lees] break up and go to Vietnam

[The Lor grandpas. Nhia Vue and Fai Do broke up.], that's just because both were trying to become mayor. Nothing big made them break up.

So that's why the Lees took over and became mayor. That's Mayor Chong Tau's position. They took over his job and gave it to Pin Ya Bee, Tou Bee Ly Fong. And he's the one that took over. They said Mayor Bee. That is Chong Tou's mayor.

Why the Hmong get a lead in our country Laos once was because they are fighting over the position of mayor and chased the

Nor Chia Lor holding a musical instrument called a *Qeej*.
Sandra Shackelford Collection, University of Wisconsin-Green Bay, Archives Department.

Lor Clan to Vietnam. Then the Japanese came. That's why our country is falling into two parts. The Hmong that went into Vietnam, that's Grandpa Nhia Vue and Fai Do and Chia Fong Lor. Those are the people who moved to Vietnam.

They are the first government people [officials]. They're the ones the French appointed to govern. They moved to Vietnam then they started the war. Fighting our country [Laos]. That's what's important. And when we're big and grown up at the time, they take big taxes. If anyone who's going to be a French soldier or soldier for the Lee Clan, then we're free of taxes. That's why we all joined the war. All the orphan boys and us. We joined because we had no money to pay the tax to them. That's why we are able to live. If we don't become soldiers, we can't live.

That's why it first started the war. And that's why we all became Red soldiers with the French. We had fought the Vietnamese [in] World War I. We fought everywhere. People have died all over. And there is war ever since.

When I was in the war, I was not able to shoot a gun yet. I only carried the powder bag and follow them around just so I am freed of taxes. Not just that. After that, there comes World War II. I will not explain the long way. I will just express this in a fast way because the cassette will not be enough. World War II started. Vietnam had fought wars again. This time, it's the "real" Vietnam War.

The first time [was] the Japanese took over our country in 24 hours. In 24 hours! Japanese had captured all the French in our country in just 24 hours! They had cut their ears [off]. Each French person, they cut one side of their ear away. And we have French person that is with us all the time. He is a sergeant. That one, the Japanese had cut one side of his ear also. After that, all of our kids are grown up and the war starts again. That's when this French guy came back. We saw that he lost his one ear and we asked him why did he lose one ear and he said because the Japanese cut it off. The French people that had ears cut off. They have a lot of them in France now because the Japanese had tortured them.

After this, the French stayed until their time is up because they had signed their time limit and their time was up. They had discussed this over in…[inaudible] the government had said if their time is up, they have to go back. That means they have to move back to France and go back to their country.

During this time, the French had moved back and Laos had

formed a group. When they had formed a group of soldiers. The Vietnamese had not gone back to their country. At first when they discussed the time limit, they had told everyone to go back. There's nothing to do with Laos anymore. The French had gone back, but the Vietnamese didn't. Because when Laos had a group of soldiers, So Va Na [the leader of the Democracy group in Laos], he's on our side. And Su Pa Na Vong lived in Vietnam and he's on the Vietnamese side. And they both are Laos. The one in Laos is Laotion, and the one in Vietnam is Laotian.

And then, at the time, the Americans had gone down to the southern part of Vietnam. That's when the Americans shook the Hmong's hand and asked us to help them block Road Number Six in North Vietnam, the main road to South Vietnam.

They said if we help them block this and if they win, the Americans will help us build our country and help our economy, and help us with taxes and everything. They will help us. They will help fix it to be as good for us as in their country. This is why General Vang Pao watched over us because at the time, Pa Na… [inaudible]. When Vang Pao came and took over, he had not been appointed a general yet. Vang Pao was doing this with us until the day he became general. He was an ordinary soldier. That's why we accepted the promise of the Americans. The Americans said, "Your country is right on the main road to Vietnam. If you all help and use guns and knives to help us block the main road between South Vietnam and North Vietnam, there will be peace in South Vietnam. So that the North Vietnam can't fight the South. When the South gets peace, then your country will be helped and be a better country like America."

"And if we lose or do not win the battle, then we shake hands and we will help your people go to America. No matter how they look. Even if you are blind and crippled, we will take you into our country." And that's why we have promised and shook hands with the American government. I forget the president that promised us. The only president I remember is Nixon.

So everybody went in and help the Americans. That's why the Americans sent in weapons, airplanes, bombs, and ammunition to our country. For the Hmong, no matter if they are big or small, just so they could hold on to a gun. We all went in and blocked the road between North and South Vietnam.

That is why people died. The people that don't have a husband and wife and children. They died all over. Just because all of us helped the Americans in the Vietnam War.

We had fought like this for at least 30, 40 years. So then, we lost a lot and the Americans said, "Now that we can't win, we will have to go back to America. But we will keep our promise."

That's why our people are here in America today— to study and to have freedom because we have the right to come to this country. And that's why we are here today. Because the American government had accepted all of us. They tell us to come because our country had been ruined. That's the promise the Americans made us when we helped them with North Vietnam. Just so the Americans could fight the North Vietnamese.

They said, when there is a country, they will come and help us build our country. And when there is no country, they will take us in. And now, to let the Hmong or the Americans, not just the ordinary people but all the government in all the cities and all the states, young and old; all the researchers, to know and to see the promise that the Americans had made us. That's why the Hmong people are here.

We are here in America for a reason and we have a reason to be here. Because the president of this country told us to come. Because ours had become communist to the Vietnamese.

Part II

Oral Histories
and Folktales

A Story of Survival

Da Thao

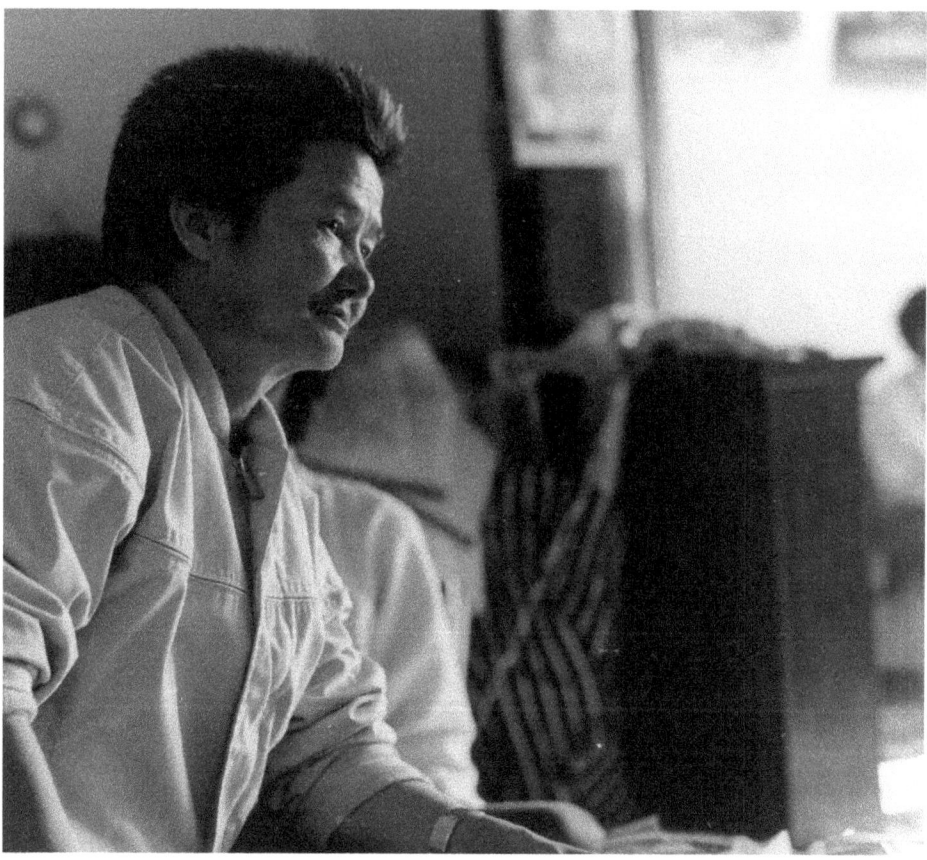

The Shaman, Mai Yang's husband, Da Thao. He assists her in her healing ceremonies.
Sandra Shackelford Collection, University of Wisconsin-Green Bay, Archives Department.

We ran from place to place. We were very poor. They killed both of my parents. All the remaining belongings on your body were taken away. You had nothing left on you. Everywhere you turn to, you hear gunshots. I had nothing to value with me that I could look forward to that would help me or anyone else. All I could see was myself running from place to place. So afraid. Holding onto my dear life.

Then they took my parents away to be killed. It was the second day. They took them away to be killed. The gunshots went off again and again and again. Tomorrow we, the three of us, arrive there. When they saw us, they began shooting at us. Like we all said, we were very fortunate and lucky. The three of us.

Leaves on the trees shattered and bullets whistled right past your eyes and ears.

Leaves on the trees shattered and bullets whistled right past your eyes and ears. We kept running. We kept running. If we didn't run, we were sure they were going to get us. We continued to run while they were shooting bullets right behind our tails. We were very scared. We decided to run back. It was about two or three days when my sister-in-law and my brother escaped from them. It was about seven days later when my younger brother escaped. Then they transported us, and that's when we decided to go and seek help.

We ran [from] place to place. We worked in a rice field with someone so my younger brother could have food. They kept on firing. We were very poor. We didn't have the chance to get any rice out in the fields. They fired gunshots at you. Rice fields and crops were ready. You were too scared to go out in the fields to get any rice to make food. One night we slept by the foot of the mountains. One night we slept in the mountain valleys. We were very poor. We ran [from] one place to another. We kept on running. As for my parents, they killed them. You run here and they still shoot at you. We were very poor. Our rice supply was lost. The things on our back, small things; money and everything on our back. They stripped it all. They took it all. They're never going to give it back.

Then we came to Thailand. We then knew how to live and then that's how we found our way. When we arrived in your country, America, we didn't have to go and patrol the surrounding areas. When we were in Thailand and Laos, we had no peaceful sleep, therefore we couldn't patrol our surrounding areas. We were very poor. We've been running. Very scared. They used airplanes to shoot at us. The airplanes shot and hit our son-in-law. A Xiong's son-in-law died. There was dirt all over me. I was very lucky. My mom and dad, they had killed them. I was the only one left. There is still the heavens above. They have the eyes. They left me.

They parachuted bombs down on me. I was covered in dirt. Bombs exploded everywhere. Dirt flew all over. BOOM! BOOM! Blood was all over but I was left. I didn't die. That is what I'm going to say. As for my mom, my dad. They killed them dead. I am the only one left.

The heavens have eyes. That's why the heavens left me to live and that's why they left me.

If you had no wrongdoings or any way to fault or no curse, that's why, when they shoot, they couldn't hit you. It's just like, when it exploded, it didn't get me. That's what I'm going to tell you. You wanted me to say it.

Then, we ran from place to place. We were their target. They flew planes in the air. They shot. We were very poor. I had the will to live. If I was cursed or something, then maybe I would have been dead. If they shot at me, it would have hit me. I would have died then. Like I said, my mom, my dad... They were slaughtered.

They were killed. They left me... That's why I was left to live. If I didn't know any form of writing and that's why... oh... They killed my mom and dad. They left me to stay. The planes shot. They parachuted the bombs. It didn't hit me. I was very poor. And you wanted me to tell it to you. This is what I'm going to tell you. We went. Then the planes started shooting. They shot. BOOM! They shot at the people ahead of me and the ones running behind me and the ones coming at me. Dirt was all over me. I started to pat my shirt, my back, my head. All full of dirt and all over. It didn't hit me. I didn't die. I was very fortunate and lucky. That's why I didn't die.

We just came and saw your place. Your country. We went and then they took us. And then we went, and they captured us. They took us and tied us up with our hands tied behind our backs. We were very heart-broken. If they were to shoot... at me... they told them not to shoot because we are the government's people. "If we are the government's people?" Then they were going to hand me to them. They let me go. Then I went for the bomb under the pillow. I almost let it go. Let it go this time so when I die, they die. I was thinking that maybe I will be the only one left. Then me... Allow them ten nights to sleep, but don't allow yourself to fall asleep so you can escape. That's when I let go. When they thought of that, too. They didn't let it go. That's why I didn't die.

If I was to let it go, we all would have been dead. There wouldn't be me now. Then one night, allow them ten nights to sleep so I could free myself. Then they took some ropes and used the ropes to tie us. They took us and passed us through all the people. Then they took us to a place to sleep. Then they tied us again. Our hands were swollen and in pain. It hurt tremendously. We told them that it was hurting too much. So they came and untied us but tied us together with the ropes under our arms. When they were asleep… They slept and fell asleep.

I sighed. If I don't escape, I'm not going to see my wife and my kids. So I untied myself and ran. I ran and escaped free. If I didn't untie it, I would have been dead. That's why I untied it. That's why I am free and I am back to see my wife and my kids. I am very happy. You wanted me to tell. This is what I have told and it's very heartbreaking. It's very upsetting. I don't know what to do. My country was intruded, [we] ran from place to place and the kids [were] all crying because they want to eat. No such thing as rice. No such thing as meat. One night, make one house. One day, make one house. But all I see is houses built from one range of hills to one range of valleys. We kept on running up and down the hills and valleys. We were very poor. There was always something that we had to run from. Not one thing that we didn't have to run from. Everywhere you turn, carry your luggage. One night, sleep. One night, build house. When almost completed, everyone said, "Run!"

It was very poor. Then we kept on running, carrying our kids on our back. Going from place to place. And it was very poor. The reason why we came to your country here, is because we have been running in and out of the wonderous mountains and hills plus we didn't have [anything] to cook and eat. If you go and start cooking, people who ride the planes above will see the field. They will rush a lot of people to come and patrol. They shot. BOOM! BOOM! Coming to you. You can't stay though. So you run. If you don't run, they will tie you up. They will kill you. That's why you run. You run and you are free. They will kill you. That's why you run. You run and you are free.

**They will kill you. That's why you run.
You run and you are free.**

The Way of Neeb

Mai Yang

Mai Yang is a Shaman of her people. As she says, it isn't something she learned; it is something given to her. She is assisted in performing many Hmong rituals and ceremonies by her husband, Da Thao. The photographs in this section of oral histories were taken at a healing ceremony at their home.

Mai performing a Hmong ritual.
Sandra Shackelford Collection, University of Wisconsin-Green Bay, Archives Department.

This is the narration of Mai Yang. She has spoken directly on tape. She is a Shaman, a woman who heals the soul and, sometimes, the body. Her husband, Da Thao, assists her in her shamanic healing rituals. The following narration describes the healing process, the calling of the Spirits to heal the person. Mai is the go-between. She transverses the Spirit World and the physical world.

When she first described going into trance to me, I thought of an old camera... the photographer bends, his head moving under a black cloth. An image is projected inside that dark, closed space. I thought of Mai Yang and the ritual I observed in this way. She'd gone inward to contact the healing Spirit — Kev Neeb —the way of Neeb, pronounced neng. In her trance, the vision bounced forward like those projected through the camera lens. Mai talks to the spirits. She banters with them. Compromises. She convinces them of the worthiness of the person seeking healing. She, as shaman, suspended for a time between two worlds, does whatever she can to get the Spirit to act in the best interest of the afflicted person.

Mai, the shamanic healer, speaks:

I'm going to talk about *Kev Neeb* [the shamanic way] and the beliefs of the spirits. I'm going to talk about *Kev Neeb* and the beliefs of the spirits. Only this one, I'm going to tell to you. I'm going to talk and tell about the way of *Ua Neeb* [perform shamanism].

Sandy told me to tell about what I see and how I heal. It's not like a *Dab* [ghost, devil, demon] that's right there so you can see [it]. But the heavens permitted it. So they only tell it to you, only in your heart and soul, to the world and to the people.

As we heal, we heal according to our Hmong culture — the Hmong culture that was left to us by our great ancestors. This was their way of leading and making the meal. It has always been like this, when the heavens created this world 'til now.

Now it's our turn. It's like this. I'm going to tell it to you. I'm just going to tell about me, myself as a whole. I don't know what it's like for others to do that. But it's like your children. When you ask a favor, you tell them to go for real and hurry, with you on the end, or to the fields or anywhere, but always be with you. It's like your child. If you can take it with you, they can go. When they go, they go in as a couple of groups. It's like when they're not going. If you *Ua Neeb, Ua Yaiv* [a shaman diagnoses the cause of illness or misfortune for the sick person] during this time, you're saying one word after another. If the *Dab* is not taking you, then you wouldn't know what to do then either.

It's not like I want to *Ua Neeb*. The ones that want to *Ua Neeb* and are listening to others do it are just the ones that are learning. The ones like us, others... I have seen that the man... some of them, day or night, they do it so much as if they were learning how to heal spiritually. But I'm telling you about myself as a whole. As for me, I couldn't learn it. One reason is because my *Sue Hue* here tells you when you prepare for *Ua Neeb*, when you get ready to do it, you are going to call like this. One minute he would say, "Do what I do. I will tell [you]." Then when you get ready to do it, you forget what he has told you to do and you don't know your *Sue Hue's* instructions when he told you what he wanted exactly for you to do.

When you are ready to *Ua Neeb*, you do it according to what your *Da Neeb* tells you and your great ancestors. Your great ancestors, whatever they do, however they do it, whatever they teach, that's how you do it. You do and follow it exactly like it. As for me, in all my life of *Ua Neeb*, I never learn a single word or heard of a single word meaning like this word. They call it like this and then you could call it exactly like them.

It's like this when I'm on the stand. Anyway, the *Dab* takes me. Whatever he does, then that's what I do. Like I said, I haven't learn a single word to use it and do it. My *Neeb* here, to this age, I have *Ua Neeb* to this old age, from since when I only had one child.

Up 'til now, this old and I haven't learned that single word to do it. Because, whatever or whoever I have healed, they have been getting better and well. But now, I haven't learned one word that the *Dab* has truly told me in my heart and soul, saying this, "You go and heal and make better," or "The *Dab* is named like this."

"You go and heal or cure this type of illness or sickness." It's like when you *Ua Neeb*, you have to reach it, then they teach you. Then you can do it and you can heal. When it's good, it's as if you have removed their pain physically. When it's not good, there's nothing they can do. They couldn't help you. They didn't help you. They didn't go with you. Maybe because you bye-bye them call the *Klua Neeb* [the shaman spirits]. Bye-bye. One word after another. They didn't take you in that much and they didn't teach you much. Then what you know, think that's what they have told you. If you didn't know it at all, then you will go and watch it back and forth. You wouldn't know what to do.

It's like a trail [maze]. You have to decide which way to go. Are you going to go and see where the trail ends? Go straight? Or make a turn? Then they're not telling you or leading you anymore. When you get there, it's like when you are traveling in the real world. When you get there, the trail has a dead end. Then you don't know what to do. It's also like in Laos.

When I got started with *Neeb*, I'm going to tell you that. The important thing is that I am able to heal my family successfully. One of my oldest daughters now living in Thailand, she is one person that was possessed by a *Dab*, a *Mo Shane* [no tranlation available] from the heavens.

One reason why I am able to heal is that my *Da Neeb* [shaman spirits] took me straight to it and was able to get my kids, my kids here, my two kids for me. That's why I could seal this *Mo Shane* here. This *Mo Shane* a long time ago was very poor. When you talk about this *Dab* here, no one responded to you a single word. The reason is because they said this *Mo Shane,* for you to be able to heal, it takes 12 karat gold for it to be healable. Right now, my *Dab* took me and told me about my two kids. It's like they were in a pot of boiling water. I went and successfully got them out. That's how I was able to heal this child of mine.

Then, since that part afterwards, I was still dumb. I'm just a woman. I'm still dumb. Then now, I didn't listen to my *Neeb's* words. My *Neeb*, my *Sue Hue*, told me to avoid. If it was me, my *Sue Hue* was supposed to avoid my house. They should not come. But I didn't listen. I was thinking that my mom would be broken hearted because it was time to cultivate the crops. So we went and cultivated the crops. It's like I didn't avoid it. Then my *Dab Neeb* got angry. That's why my child got sick. My son got real sick and died. This is one thing that I could not heal. I could not help my child. That's why I lost this child. It's like, after that, and so on forth, that when I knew that maybe to heal, to heal the *Dab*, I had to heal it like this to be successful.

It's like fixing a *Tooj Kwj*. You have to go straight up to the *Tooj Kwj* for you to fix it successfully. *Kev Neeb* [the way of Neeb], *Kev Yaib*, I told about *Kev Neeb*. It's like that, what other people say when they dream. Me? I'm not dreaming.

Wherever the *Dab* took me to go and heal, that's all I can tell. It's not like my eyes have seen it. Other people, I don't know what they see, but me, I don't see. Whatever the *Dab* looks like, I don't see. The *Dab*, the one you go to heal, you don't see. But the heavens didn't expose them for you to see — meaning — this *Dab* looks like this. I can't tell you. Me. Myself. Since I have been doing this, I haven't seen the *Dab*. If it's big or if it's small, I can't tell it to you. I'll truly tell you that

Kev Neeb, Key Yai [a shaman diagnoses the cause of illness or misfortune of the sick person]. The *Dab* is named like this. You can go and heal it this way. The [angel] takes you. Then go and compromise to the area of sickness. Then you go and heal that. Then it will be better.

Maybe if your *Neeb* goes and finds it, your *Neeb* says, "Maybe your spirit went and wants to reincarnate." One thing, you could go and heal it. Sometimes when you do it, you go and maybe the spirit has gone or reached its burial ground. There's a lot of them. One of them is the grave. When you have reached that far, you go and wake them and compromise. Then you can heal it.

Next time, when they wish for you to go and heal, you heal that,

Decorations in Mai's home.
Sandra Shackelford Collection, University of Wisconsin-Green Bay, Archives Department.

and you will be able to heal that one particular problem. Finish one solution like this. One reason more to add on. If you are to go and heal the *Dab Poj Ntxoog* [referring to a girl or woman ghost], the *Dab's* relatives, *Dab's* girlfriend and boyfriend, you will not see how any of these *Dab* look like.

What does it look like? Does it look like a human? You will not see. But your *Dab Neeb* can see. But they will not tell you and say, "Your

Dab Neeb is that one." They tell it in your heart, saying, "You heal this. You block this." Then it must be done. Then that's all you do. You heal it. Then it's well.

I have healed many before. I am not boasting. But you wanted me to tell it. Then I must describe it according to what I have healed successfully. The ones that are real sick and not making any progress, other people have said that they are sure to die. Sometimes, when I go and heal, they got well. Others say, give him or her three days. Maybe he or she will die. You don't have to *Ua Neeb* anymore because he or she will die anyway.

I have healed that, too, because I do go and just heal. I am not like the others. When you get there, [they] get furious, compromise and block them. I don't do that. I go slowly and compromise with them. Bribe them. And if we agree with you, then you can separate people to people and *Dab* to *Dab*. Then you *Hauj* [compromise] it and then you can heal it. If you can turn them and succeed at bribing, then you can turn around and [the person that is sick] will come back to reality out here.

That's how you can heal. Others, when you get there, if it's the "wild" *Dab* or the *Dab Tshob Tshua*, [a ghost that causes sleep paralysis] then they are stubborn. When you get there, you slap papers vigorously at them. You be the big one. You act real tough to it. At this time, the reason why you could not heal [is] because, when they get there, they act tough to them and slapped papers at them. Slam your hands. Slam your feet and you yell at them. Then they get mad, and they refuse. It's like that.

The way of *Ua Neeb* just goes like this. There is no one that has done it and save the *Dab*. If it looks like a human or a *Dab*. See how the *Dab* looks like. Never saw it. We did *Neeb* this old, that we never knew. For example, when you do it, you go and heal this time. Then they took the Angel Spirit and locked it up in their rock and metal cells. They saw that the person, they took it and did this to them. Then, this is what you need to heal so the person can get well. It's just like that. They do tell. It's like a child. When you take a child and tell that this is that, and this is this. It's like your teachers. When the child goes to school, the teacher says, "You will learn this to that. You will go here to there." It's just like that. The difference is that you don't see the image as a clear person, the person that comes and teaches. It is only that you are the one taking them and bye-ing [calling] them.

They tell it in your heart and soul saying, "This. You go and heal it here... the area of moaning. You go and heal it here." This is where your angel has gone to. But we, what our great ancestors have left behind, are our Hmong here. That is the reason why, to this day, Hmong never let that *Kev Neeb* and *Kev Yaib* go. Whenever you hear of a person not getting well at all, you go and do a complete *Neeb*. You *Hauj* [compromise or negotiate] it. Then the person gets all right.

It is not that we are craving for meat and we do this so we have meat to eat. The heavens have permitted us to come and heal the world. We are Hmong, this is how our culture goes. We must heal according to that.

I have told about my way of *Ua Neeb* and *Ua Yaiv*. I heal the old, the young — just as long as they have the *Yeej* [the "correct" illness]. It is always God, no doubt. If you have gone and healed but it doesn't fit in, maybe, his or her *Yeej Kong Yeej Hua* [glory by goals and achievements, honor by having high respect and high self-esteem] didn't reach it like the elders have said. They were not meant for you to heal or maybe you were not meant to heal that person. The illness was not a match. That's why your healing didn't match. Therefore, you could not heal successfully.

For example, if you *Hauj* there, and the person stands right up, almost as if it's a lie. It is like a thorn. When you remove it, then the person gets well. At that time, it is your *Dab Neeb* that is helping you and you have the *Yeej* [illness]. Your *Yeej Kong, Yeej Hua* could reach it. Then that's how you can heal successfully and get well, too.

That's not all — the healing through *Ua Neeb, Ua Yaiv*. The way of *Ua Neeb* and everything else — the *Txoj* [the burial hole], what they call the *Xwm* [already in the coffin ready to be buried], *Fab Txoj*. When you sort and get that far, your *Dab Neeb* says, "The Bad Angel truly went down there. We must go and wake it up and heal it. It must work. We are going to heal and truly *Hauj* it. It must be well."

When you go and *Hauj* there, it really gets better. For example, if the Angel Spirit — the child — goes and falls down into the ground, the spirit is hurt on the ground. The spirit gets hurt, and it cannot get up. If you let *Klua Neeb* stand it up, it is not possible. If you go and *Txhaw*, it is not possible.

One reason why some people cannot do it to make a match, you let your *Klua Neeb* over here go and just wake them and *Txeej, Txeej* [calling but not doing anything to] them. That's not going to do it. Not possible. If that's so, our Hmong, our Hmong culture, the reason we never let *Ua Neeb* and *Ua Kev Yaiv* go was because our great ancestors have left it to us — our Hmong life. It doesn't matter what other people have said. "Just forget it!" But my *Kev Neeb, Kev Yaiv* here, *Neeb*. If I do it, it is not at fault. I am a person with a straight, pure heart. When I *Ua Neeb*, I do it for free. I do it cleanly and do it for real. I'm not cheating on anything or cheating anyone so I could get to eat. *Ua Neeb, Ua Yaiv. You Ua Neeb Ua Yaiv* to the ones that don't discriminate [against] you.

It's not like they call upon you and then you go out and do it. *Kev Neeb, Kev Yaiv*. The heavens permitted it to be done. You can't choose and say, "Oh. This person. I wish to help and then I will help. I don't want to help, then I will not help." It's not like that. My *Kev Neeb, Kev Yaiv* helps relatives and friends. Yet, we don't know one another. When they came and arrived, I went and did *Neeb* to help them. If they had the heart to ask for help, I was happy to help them. Truly. To heal anyone, anywhere, is good.

It is not as if you are going to see someone or something in front of you, giving you instructions or leading your way. There is no such thing.

I am going to say this to you. When you play it to listen, you, the one that is listening, you listen. Either, if you type it into the computer, I'm telling you. Type it correctly like the way I have said it. Whether you are going to play it to listen. I have spoken it clearly.

A traditional Hmong table setting.
Sandra Shackelford Collection, University of Wisconsin-Green Bay, Archives Department.

One thing: the way of *Ua Neeb, Ua Yaiv,* and the *Ntsuj Plig* Spirit don't choose. Unlike *Yaiv* [gets better and then worsens again] and the Angel, the Spirit goes in reincarnate. Maybe the spirit went back to our ancestors. I'm saying this: it is like the spirit's way to reincarnate. The Spirit [is trying to find a way] to go and invade a sickness. If they come and ask for me to help, I could still heal it. It is still possible to heal. One thing. Maybe they don't have the *Yeej* or they are just looking for *Kev Chia* [for the illness]. I can still heal it. I heal only what I can heal. It is not like, if I can heal it, then I've got to boast and say, "I can heal!" If it is healable, then I say I can heal. If it is not healable, then I say, "I can't heal." Now, the side that I first spoke into was side 1. I will tell my son to mark on it. The one that is already done is me, telling stories. But on the side *Ua Neeb*, I recorded and messed it up. I recorded the stories but there was one side left. I couldn't record anything so then there's one side left.

I again recorded a story. There's still [some] l left. The story was not done yet. Then I recorded on the other side. Then, I spoke in confusion and mixed up. Now, *Kev Neeb*. That was all I'm going to say.

I don't know what to tell. I didn't see a single *Dab*. See how it looks like so I don't know what to tell. This is all I'm going to tell. *Kev.* The way of *Neeb*. I heal all friends and relatives. I heal according to what I have said. Everyone must know you, *Ua Neej*, what it is like and what you see. What you will see and will not see. They only tell it in your heart and soul. You close your eyes to get there. Open your eyes and you are still just sitting there. You borrow their mouth to speak.

You only borrowed their mouths to talk and converse with them. Just calling them. I haven't seen anything. I am just telling you the way of *Ua Neeb*, the way of *Ua Yaiv*. Everyone, evidently everyone, has done it along the same road. Evidently, it is all the same. Doesn't matter what anyone says. So long as you don't go and learn and do *Neeb* the evil way. I'm going to say it purely to the heavens that I only do *Neeb* the way the heavens permitted me to do. I never do more. I never do it any differently. This is all I'm going to say to you. The other side isn't done yet. This side, I have only spoken about halfway or just about middle. I'll see what happens.

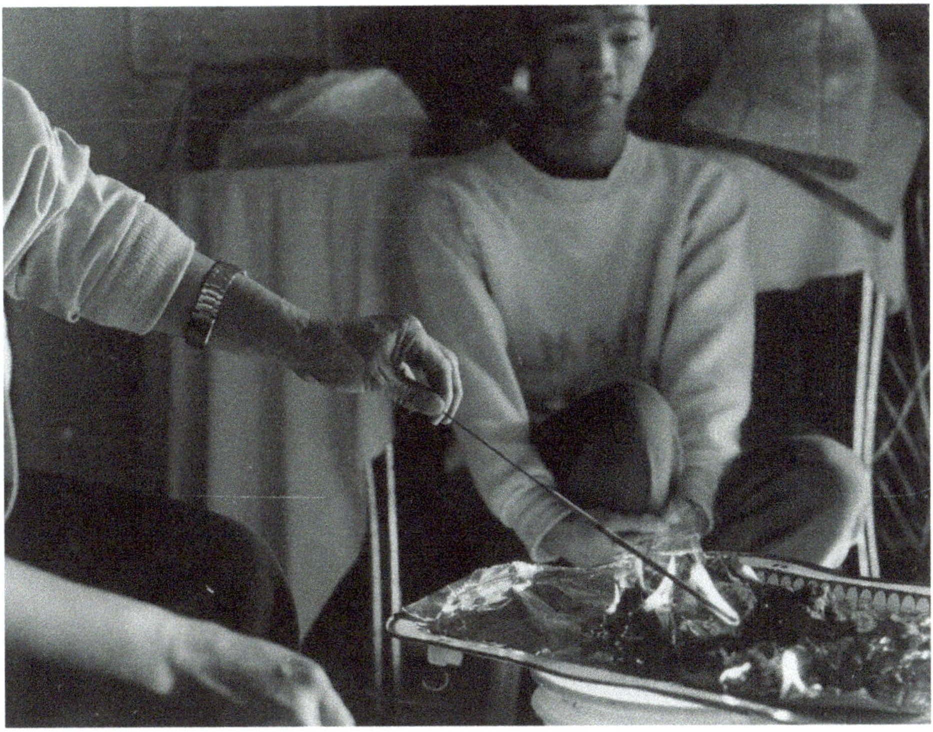

Da Thao assisting his shamanic wife [Mai Yang] in a healing ceremony.
Sandra Shackelford Collection, University of Wisconsin-Green Bay, Archives Department.

Glossary of Shamanic Terms

Dab: ghost, devil, demon

Daj paj txoo: ghost

Dab poj ntxoog: referring to a girl or woman ghost

Dab Neeb: shaman spirits

Dab tshob tshua/ Dab tsog tsuag: a ghost that causes sleep paralysis

Fab: weedy

Hauj/ Haum: compromise

Keb neeb Kev Yaig/ kev neeb kev yaig: he shamanic way (ways of healing and integrating the body, mind, and spirit or life force, as well as providing wisdom through direct experience.)

Kev Chia: for the illness

Kev Caiv: prohibits or culturally confines someone into the home for a few days.

Kev Neeb [the way of Neeb]: the shamanic way

Kev Neeb: human way

Klua Neeb/ Qhua Neeb: shaman spirits

Kwj: valley

Neeb: shamanism

Ntsuj Plig: soul

Sue Hue/ Xib fwb: master or teacher

The ntsuj plig spirit/ Ntsuj plig: is normally referring to a soul and not the spirit

Toj: hill

Txeej: calling but not doing anything to them

Txheej: level of the spiritual realm

Txheev: call or request (the shaman spirits)

Txoj: referring to something long and thin (like road or thread)

Ua Neeb [the doing]: perform shamanism

Ua Yaiv/ Ua Yaig: a shaman diagnoses the cause of illness or misfortune of the sick person

Xwm: matter or bad news (note from transcriber: According to the above story, I think it's more like a **Xyw**: it sounds spirit of the dead)

Yeej huam: honor by having high respect and high self-esteem

Yeej koob: glory by goals and achievements,

Folktales

Orphan and the Ghost

As told by Mai Yang

Then Orphan and Ger's mom and dad, they died and left Orphan and Ger to stay [behind on the earth] Ger and Orphan, they stayed til they were grown. Then Orphan went and married a wife. Orphan arrived on the path and said, "Ah. We are thirsty. Since we are here, I'll, ah… You stay here and I'll go and carry water for us to drink."

Orphan's wife sat on the path while Orphan went and carried the water. Three *Poj Ntxoog* [ghosts who are recently deceased] *Hu Hu Dab* [eat like pigs]. They arrived on the path and said, "You marry her husband and we'll eat her." Then Orphan's wife stayed. When Orphan came back with the water, two of the *Poj Ntxoog* took it [the wife] and ate it under a cliff. Finish it. Then they let one of them come and marry Orphan. When they arrived at home the *Poj Ntxoog* went and bit the town's chicken and pigs to eat. Orphan went farming every day. *Poj Ntxoog* [the ghost] stayed at home and ate the town's chicken and pigs. Orphan didn't know.

Every day, Orphan went farming. [Orphan asks] "Why? The town? One day, one whole family moves. Where are you guys going?" "We're going to go sleep at the farm. Go. Gather your chickens and pigs and stay at the farm. We're to live at the farm."

Then, the *Poj Ntxoog* was *Hu Hu Dab*. *Poj Ntxoog* was left. *Poj Ntxoog* [the ghost] was a woman so she was just a *Poj Ntxoog*. She ate all the chicken and pigs. The whole town was afraid. One day, one family moved. The whole town was almost cleared. Orphan's wife was a hog! She ate everyone's chickens and pigs! Killed and ate it all! Then they said, "Ah. All right then. We're going to go and sleep at the farm. Um… We're going to go for a couple of days and we will return." They went to sleep. They went to farm. They all left. All the townspeople all left. Orphan looked.

Everyday we went farming. Come home and all the townspeople were cleared… gone. Then Orphan went and asked an oracle. Ger said Ger wanted to go, too. Then Orphan said, "You don't go. Uh… you stay. You stay and I'll go only. I'll run. I'll run there and I will return." Then Orphan ran. Orphan ran there. Ran there and took a red-eyed dog. Tied the male horse in his stable. Then said, "You stay. If you are afraid. I'll lock you in. I'll run quickly there and I will return." Orphan sealed the stable and locked Ger in it. The tiger, the *Poj Ntxoog*, already came and undid it and came in and already ate Ger up. When Orphan arrived there, he asked the Oracle and said, "Oracle. Why did all the townspeople run away?"

[The Oracle responded:] "Orphan. Um… The reason why the townspeople ran away is because your wife is not who she is. Your wife, when you guys arrived on the path, three *Poj Ntxoog*, they ate her up. They told the two older sisters to eat her. The two older sisters told the younger sister to come and marry you. Your wife, they already ate her. What's left? This one is just a *Poj Ntxoog*. Then finished the town's chicken and pigs. Ate all the chicken and pigs. The townspeople were afraid. That's why they all left. That's why you're the only [one] left. You're the only one that didn't know. Right now, you. You hurry. Your sister at home, that will be the end of her!"

Oh! Orphan and Orphan's red-eyed dog. They went back home. Ran home and then arrived at home. Then… why… Ger was all eaten up. Ger was not seen around.

"Ah," [wonders Orphan]. "Where did Ger go?"

[The ghost speaks:] "Eh… Ger went to pick some vegetables."

[Orphan:] "If that's right, go and call Ger back."

[The ghost] went out onto the front porch and said, "Ger. Hurry. Come back. Orphan came back. So hurry and come back." Ger didn't hear.

[Orphan speaks] "Standing right there, how is she to hear? Better go over there to the mountains. Then she'll hear."

Then the *Poj Ntxoog* run over to the mountain. Calling. Fading into the distance. Then the rooster said, "Cloe. Cloe. Cloe. You feed me the rice and I'll tell you." He grabbed a hand full of corn. Finished it. Wiggled and all shaken up. The hands. The feet. The head. The stomach and the intestines all came up.

Orphan was very mad. Then Orphan said [to the chicken], "I'm gonna go. You don't come onto the ground. You stay up on the tree. And, uh… the red-eyed dog. The red-eyed dog can go. So he'll go with me and my horse. I'm going to lock him up in the stable."

He locked up the male horse in the stable and the rooster flew away to stand high up in the tree. Then he took his red-eyed dog and ran. Ran and ran. He went and reached a town and never came back. Then one group. One group arrived, moved into this town. They didn't know. So they came to sleep. They slept in that town. Then the *Poj Ntxoog* came and said, "You guys. Our town has a lot of meat [animals, livestock]. You watch your livestock carefully before they will be sorry. [If they get] stuck in the thorns and be sorry."

So then, they took apart their house to make a big opening in the fence for their animals: the chickens, the pigs, the cows, and the buffalo. Then, later at night, she [the Ghost] came to bite their pigs. The pigs began to squeak. They started to shoot. Then she ran back to her house and stayed up there and said, "People. Don't shoot. You might hit me. Shoot! Shoot somewhere else. Don't shoot this way. Shoot over there." So they went back to sleep. She then came back again. She pulled on the pig's feet and the pigs started squeaking again. They started shooting at it. Then she started running back to her house and said, "People! Don't shoot over here. It might hit me. Shoot over there."

Then, they went out and set string traps. They went and watched it. Her [the ghost's] eyes were bulged out. She was very small. They set out string traps. Then they all went to sleep again. In just a moment, she came back to get the pigs and got trapped. "Oh, hurry!" "Why? What are you doing out here?"

"Ah... I came out here to piss, but I got stuck on these strings here or got trapped in something."

They they tied her up with her hands behind her back. They started to beat on her. They kept on beating and beating and beating. Then they tied her to the tree. Tied her on the tree with her hands behind her back to stay out in the sun.

Then, tomorrow in the morning, they released the male horse from the [barn] to come and carry the luggage. "People. The male horse is my husband's horse. You do not use it to carry the luggage."

They wanted to use the male horse to carry the luggage but she wouldn't let them because it was her husband's horse. Then they said they didn't know. It was theirs. They were going to let it carry the luggage and go. Then, they just [fix] it to carry the luggage and left.

The horse carrying the luggage arrived at the husband. Her, she was left behind, tied to the tree with her hands behind her back. Tied to the tree. Left on the tree to stay. When the horse arrived… when it got there, he said, "Oh. The horse there belongs to me. Why did you use it to carry luggage to come here?"

"Oh. We didn't know that this horse belongs to you. But when we arrived at this small town, there was a very small woman who lived in the town. She had bulgy eyes. And she said that the town had [animals that eat your animals]. We took down our house[s] to fence in the animals. We took down our house[s] to fence in the animals. Then she came to steal. She grabbed our pigs and our pigs squealed. Then we went out to set a trap. We then trapped her. We got her. Then we tied her and tied her to a tree, to a stake, tying her to stay out in the sun. We didn't release her."

"Oh! If that's right, then thank you. Ah. If you succeed in tying her up, then you take me back. That horse is my horse, but she has already eaten my wife. Then she came and married me. I'm going to tell you. Go back with me."

Then he went back. When he arrived there, she said, "Daddy... Why did you go so long? I am very hungry. They tied me. They beat me and I'm very hungry. Come and release me."

"Okay. I'm going to rest until I have gotten enough rest." He came and rested for a long time.

"Release, Daddy. I'm very hungry. Release."

"Okay. Let me eat lunch." He finished eating.

"Go ahead and release, Daddy."

Then the husband came and started beating her. After beating and beating and beating her, he said, "You. You *Poj Ntxoog*. You finished eating my wife, then where did you put her? Tell. If you are not going to tell, I'll kill you right then."

"Oh. I apologize. It wasn't me who ate her. It was my two older sisters that ate her. They ate your wife then they told me to come and marry you. That's why I decided to come with you. But they ate her and took her to stay under the cliff. I'll go and I'll take you there."

When they arrived on the path, the *Poj Ntxoog* called and said, "Two older sisters. Ah! You finished eating their wife. Now you tell them to marry someone else. Now they are going to kill me. You have come and risen [free them of the trouble] their way to them. Risen their wife to them. Then it will be fine. If not that, then I will surely die."

Then the two older sisters came. They came and went to the place under the cliff and led them to the cliff. Oh my! Orphan connected the head. Gathered the hands and feet and connected them. Gathered the bones and connected it to a finish. Then the two *Poj Ntxoog* came and one blew the upper body from the head, and one blew the lower half from the feet. One blew three blows. The other blew three blows. After they finished blowing, the muscles started to form. The muscles formed and covered the completed body. They blew again. The older sister blew three times into the foot. After blowing into her, the wife came back to life again. She stood straight up and said, "The two that ate me are them two. And the one that came and married you is that one there."

Then the husband got real angry and said, "You. You *Poj Ntxoog* here are too evil. I have to kill you to show you. You are too evil." Then he killed the younger sister to show the older sisters. The older sisters got real scared and ran away. They have risen the Orphan's wife back to Orphan. Orphan took her back and then they went on and made a living.

The Frog, the Crab, and the Muskrat

As told by Mai Yang

Orphan's older brother didn't love Orphan. They were very poor so Orphan said, "Oh! All right then. I'll go and trap some birds."

Then Orphan went ahead and trapped birds… Orphan went all day, went and trapped birds all day till dark and got two bags. Orphan took the birds home and started to clean them. Cleaned and cleaned and cleaned till dark. Frogs and crabs and muskrats came. The frog came and said, "My dear Orphan, we are very hungry. If you don't give birds for us to eat them, please, give us the stomachs and the intestines for us to eat."

"Ah! My dear frog. How much could you possibly eat? If you want to eat, then come here and I'll give you some to eat. A stomach full of waste! What are you going to eat it for?"

Orphan handed some to the frog then he left. A moment later, the muskrat came and said, "My dear Orphan, we are very hungry. Please, if you don't give meat for us to eat, then pleast give us the stomach and intestines for us to eat. If there is anything, please, you call on us and we'll help."

"Ah! My dear muskrat. If you are hungry then I will give a stomach of waste. What are you going to eat it for?"

Then Orphan handed some for the muskrat to eat and away he went with it. Then, later, the crab came. The crab came and said, "My dear Orphan, we are very hungry. Please, if you don't give us meat to eat, then please, give us the stomach and intestines to eat."

Orphan said, "My dear crab. The stomach? The intestine? What are you going to eat it for? If you want to eat, I will give. How much could you possibly eat?"

Then Orphan gave some birds to the crab and away he left with it. Orphan was cleaning his birds then it began to get dark. The Ghosts of the cemetery came. They came playing the drum… Hitting. POOM! POOM! POOM! And dancing their way to Orphan. When they got to Orphan, one said, "Orphan, let's fight. If you beat us then we'll give you our silver and gold to you. If you don't win, then we'll eat you." Orphan said, "Fine."

Then Orphan went and called Frog, Crab and Muskrat. "Ghosts

of the cemetery are going to come and have a fight with me. If I win, they will give me silver and gold. If I lose, they will eat me."

"Okay. Go ahead. In a moment we will come and help you."

They came and fought and fought and fought. The crab clamped. The muskrat bit. The frog swallowed. They kept on with it. The ghosts of the cemetery were not winning. Then the ghosts of the cemetery said, "That's right. We're not [beating] you. Let's drink. Let's drink wine. If you drink and beat us, then we won't eat you. We'll give you our silver and gold. If you drink and don't [beat] us, then we will eat you."

"Do that. Then do that."

Then they drank. They drank wine. The muskrat and the crab. The frog was complaining but he kept swallowing. The crab, he made holes and clamped it then threw it away. And the muskrat. He kept putting holes in the cup. Then Orphan won.

"Ah! Orphan. You are good. You are too good. If that's right, then let's boil pumpkins to eat. If you win, then you get our silver and gold. If you lose, then we will eat you."

"Yes. Yes."

Then he said, "Ah! Frog and Muskrat and Crab. They said for me to boil pumpkins to eat. If I win then they will give me silver and gold. If I don't win, then they are going to eat me. What do you have-say?"

"We will come."

Then they went and boiled pumpkins. Had gone and boiled a lot of pumpkins. Crab, he was busily clamping and throwing them away. Frog was gusily swallowing it. Muskrat? He was busy making holes in it. They kept doing it. Then Orphan won.

"Ah! You beat us. Orphan, tomorrow you come here. You come here and pick up your silver and gold."

Tomorrow, when it was light, silver and gold was everywhere. Orphan had silver and gold. Then Orphan carried the birds home. When he got home, his sister-in-law said, "Orphan. What did you do? How come you have birds, silver and gold?"

"Ah! Sister-in-law. I went and trapped birds and then just got gold and silver. If you want it, then you have to go and trap birds. Go trap birds and you'll get silver and gold."

"You went and trapped birds and you got silver and gold?"

"Uh, huh! I went to go trap birds and I get silver and gold."

Then Orphan's older brother decided to go. "All right then. I'll tell you, older brother, to go. Your older brother will go and trap."

Then Orphan's older brother went. Dragging a horse with him and he went. Orphan's brother went to trap. Had gone and trapped all day. He trapped a lot, too. It was dark. Orphan's older brother cleaned and cleaned and cleaned [the birds] until dark. Crab and Muskrat came again and said, "Orphan. If you don't give meat for us to eat then, please, give us the stomach and intestines for us to eat."

"You lazy thing. If you want to eat, go and find it for yourself. I want to eat.

That's why I came here to look!" Chasing after it. Hitting it. Chasing after it. Hitting it. Hitting until the frog's legs were all broken up.

"Hmmm! He's got plenty. Didn't let us have anything. Later, he will know. We're not going to help him."

Frog was crying. Then frog left. One moment later, the muskrat came. Then he said, "Orphan. We are very hungry. Please. If you don't give us to eat then, please, give the stomachs and the intestines for us to eat."

"You fool! So lazy to go and find? I want to eat. That's why I came here to look. And now, you come and ask for me to give food for you to eat."

Chasing after it. Hitting it. Chasing after it. Hitting it. The muskrat ran and ran and ran. Then he said, "Won't give us any to eat? Then save it! Later he will know."

Then, later, the crab came. The crab came and said, "Ah! Orphan. We are very hungry. If you don't give us meat for us to eat then, please, give the stomach and intestines for us to eat."

"You foolish, lazy thing! I wanted to eat, that's why I came to look. And now, you come and beg for some[thing] to eat. I'll chase you and hit you."

Orphan chased and hit the crab. The crab's arms were all broken up. The crab was crying. "Won't give us any to eat? Then save it! Later, we will forget about helping. We are not going to help you. Later, you will know."

Oh! It was getting dark. Ghosts of the Cemetery came playing their drums. BOOM! BOOM! BOOM! Dancing their way to Orphan. When they arrived. They said, "Orphan. Let's fight!"

"Fight? Then let's fight."

Then they fought and fought and fought. And Orphan didn't win. "Uh. Now. You didn't win us. So let's drink. Drink wine." Oh! They drank. They drank wine. And Orphan lost again. He didn't win either. Then they said, "You didn't win us. Let's boil pumpkins and eat."

Then the Ghosts of the Cemetery went and started the fire to boil the pumpkins for them to eat. They had a lot of them so, one had one, another had one, and another had one. It wasn't long before it was gone. And Orphan? They finished a couple but Orphan, he didn't even finish one. Then they simply ate Orphan, too. After they finished eating Orphan, they put the bones back on the horse to carry [in its saddle-bags]. Then they loaded Orphan's bird on the horse's back to carry it back.

Oh! When the horse arrived at home, thinking that it was her husband, she went to see. She went and saw. The Ghost of the Cemetery had packed the bones in a bag to carry it back. They had loaded the horse with the bag of bones and the bag of birds. When the horse arrives at home, the story ends. I'm going to leave it like this. Maybe this is all I'm going to say. It's done. Now I'll say it in the other one.

Orphan Finds a Wife

As told by Mai Yang

A father and his son were very poor. The mother had already died and left the father and son. The two of them. The orphans. They went and worked on a field. They worked on this one field. Pumpkins were very good. The two, father and son, worked on the pumpkin [field] til it was ready to harvest. Then they went to gather the pumpkins. The father and son went and gather pumpkins. They went and gathered and got some of them. They gathered and gathered and gathered until they got to the end. And there! There was one huge pumpkin. It was one of the biggest pumpkins.

They carried the biggest one and saved it. They went on with the gathering and finished it. The father and son then came home. They ate the small pumpkins. They ate all of the small pumpkins. They ate and ate and ate and finished all the small ones. All that was left was the biggest one. Then the son said, "Dad. Let's not eat this one. Save this one. Save it until it gets really big. Save it so whenever we have a craving for it, we will eat it." That's what the son said.

Oh! The son, his name is Sakapah. Oh! They finished eating it. "Oh! Dad. Let's get the pumpkin for us to eat!"

Then the father and son were going to prepare it. When they chopped it in half, there was a boy in the pumpkin. In that big pumpkin! The boy said, "Dad. I don't have any relatives. I don't have any relatives, so why don't you raise me as a relative?"

Father and son then raised him [orphan] till grown up. As a grown up they went every day to set traps. They went out setting traps. Then they caught an elephant. It caught an elephant. They said they were going to kill it and eat it. Then the elephant said, "Ah! You want to eat. One circle cut around me. Whatever you get, that's what you'll eat." The child, the child that came out from the pumpkin, is named Pe-Wa-Kee [Pen-i]. It is called Sakapah. It is called Peni.

Then, he circled a knife around it and got a piece about as wide as the size of your hand. "Ah! If we should eat it, then it would not be enough. Then let's save it. And let it be our good luck charm. Let's put it into this jar. Let's save it." Then they put it in the jar and saved it. They went farming every day. And every day, after farming, they came home and cooked dinner. Then they said, "Ah! How come? Why? When we thank the townspeople, they would lecture. Why? Every night the townspeople made dinner ready… waiting for us."

They came and thanked the townspeople, but they were giving them trouble. They went farming. They went farming every day. And every day they came back after the townspeople had already finished cooking dinner, waiting for them. Every day, when they came home from farming, they kept on thanking them, but every day, they would get trouble from the townspeople. Then they went and asked an oracle.

"Ah. Oracle! Why? Every day we go and farm. And every day they made dinner waiting for us. Every night waiting for us. And every time we thank the townspeople, they would give us trouble. What is wrong?"

"Ah! You fill rice in a basket and you say, "We'll get a broom and sweep the house and put it away."" Then you carry your baskets and go to the fields. Go and hide upstairs. A moment later, then it will come out."

Then they took the brooms and swept the house and stored away the brooms. They went to the field and hid upstairs. Later, when it was time for people to return from the fields, there were money sounds in the bedroom. The sound was in the bedroom. Ger came out to make dinner. The sound of money came from the bedroom. Ger came and out came Ger. Ger came out… out of the jar.

Then Ger came out to look and said, "Ah! Sakapah and Peni. They used the broom to sweep the house. Where did they put it? How come I can't find it? Ah! I wonder where they put it."

Then they threw down the broom and said, "Chee-Chee. Tua Tua." Are you going to be human or *dab* [ghost]? She then flew straight into the bedroom.

She came and lived with them. The King came to town and saw Sakapah's wife. "Oh! So beautiful! What am I going to do? What am I going to do to get Sakapah's wife? Ah! What am I going to do so I get her? What should I do?"

"Ah! Go and call the Shaman to come here and you'll get it." Then they went and called the *lee-nyoog* [devil]. They went and called the devil to come and stay on the roof. Cry out once, then she got a headache. Cry out two times, then she lost her memory. Cry out three times, then she [blacked] out [dead]. Peni said, "Ah! All right then. You watch sister-in-law carefully. You don't touch sister-in-law at all. You look and watch her carefully. I will go."

Then Peni went. Peni went…went up very high [to heaven]. Just when they arrived there, his sister-in-law was already up there [in heaven]. He was very angry.

When he arrived there, the King said, "Ah! Now, who are you going to marry? Why did we send the Shaman down to earth?" That's what the King said. Then Peni said, "Ah! I'm returning back down to earth, so let me sent it [the Shaman]." [The King said:] "Oh. If you are returning back down to earth, then let us send it [the Shaman].
Peni said: "Um! Let me send it." Peni then sent it [the Shaman]. Peni sent it and arrived on the road.

"Ah, Shaman. It is tiring. Let us rest right here. Let us split bamboo to weave a basket to store them *ma kia, ma hue* [oranges and fruit]. Just in case so when we carry the *ma kia, ma hue* might fall from it [the basket]. I'm going to split these *ncuw* [bamboo] here to weave a basket."

He then weaved and weaved and weaved and finally it was done. "Ah! Shaman, why don't you crawl into here. Right. If you crawl into here and the oranges don't fall out, then you won't fall out. If you don't fall out then tell me where you can see [the hole in the basket]. Tell me and I'll patch it up. Because if we get oranges in it, it might fall out."

The Red Devil went into the basket and said, "Right here. I can see. Put one patch on it." And he patched. "Right here. I can see. Put one patch on it." Then Peni patched it. Peni patched and patched and patched till it was all completed. It was all dark. Red Devil could not see any more. "Ah. Right now. If you don't call my sister-in-law back to Earth to my brother, this time I'm going to let go and let you go from up here [in heaven] down to Earth. You will surely die."

[Red Devil said:] "Please. Please. Please. I won't do it anymore. I beg for you to take me down to Earth first. I'll go and call your sister-in-law to come back. I'll go and call your sister-in-law back and this time, I'll never do it again. Please!"

Peni took him and arrived on Earth. Then he said, "You better call my sister-in-law to come back."

Shout out one cry. She was as pale. Cry out two cry. She could hear a little more. Cry out three cries. She was alive. Cry out four cries, five cries. The one in the Heavens came down and the one on the Earth stood up. "All right then, Shaman. Where is your strongest point?" [The Shaman answered.] "My strongest point is where the color is black and beyond. [His tongue]."

"Then stick it [your tongue] out as far as possible for me to see it." He stuck it all the way out. Exposed the back area. Then he cut it off with one scissor cut.

"Right! Now why don't you call her to go back?"

"*Leea!*" That's all he said. He couldn't call any more.

"Ah! You finish cutting off my strongest spot. How am I suppose to be strong? Now I'm not strong any more."

"All right then. I'll release and let you go."

Then Peni and Sakapah released and let him go. They let him go. When he reached the heavens, the King said, "If that's right, you go back to Earth because my wife is gone. Because my wife is gone, you go back here. Please! I beg you to do it again."

"Ah! I can't do it. You did not send me. Instead you let Sakapah send me. Sent me, and when I arrived on Earth, then they cut off my tongue. They already cut off my tongue. They cut off the strongest spot. How can I possibly do it? I don't do it anymore. I can't call [the spirits] anymore." Ah! The King couldn't win her. Sakapah and Peni got her. They got her. Then they came. Sakapah got her. Then they made a living.

Then Peni said, "Ah! I'm getting old. I'm getting old. You watch. I'm going to go back. I'm not going to live with you two. You don't call me by my name. You don't call by my name and let me go. I'm going to go for real." "Uh! Today. You go. We won't say it anymore."

He left for a little while. Then the sister-in-law began to miss him so she said, "Ah! Right now I wonder how far Peni has gone?" A moment later, he ran back with his head nodding back and forth. "Ah! Sister-in-law! I told you not to call by my name. Why did you mention about me?" "Ah! I missed you so much. I totally forgot about it and said your name." Ah! A moment later. "All right then. I am gonna go. And don't mention me." They came home and stayed one day and slept one night. Then tomorrow he said, "Sister-in-law, this time I'm going to go for real now. This time, you don't mention about me at all. I'm going to go for real. It's time for me to go. I'm going to go for real." Ah! Peni went. Peni went and Peni was old. Peni was very old so Peni left. Then they stayed until they forgot about him. Oh! By the time they remembered about him, Peni had already died. Peni helped get a wife for Sakapah. They came and made a living and Peni went back [to the Other World].

The Story of the Rainbow

As told by Mai Yang

Ah! Now I'm going to tell a story. Ah! Now Orphan is telling and talking by the tree. Ah! He is very poor. He does work for the townspeople. He chops woods for the townspeople to use. Then Orphan, he lived down by the big tree. Orphan has one older brother. That one older brother... That country. That place. That town... has one tiger. A huge tiger that eats [lives] off the place, the town.

Now, the people agreed. Once a month, one family sends in one person [for the tiger to eat]. The next month, another family sends in one. Ah! They keep sending until it got to Orphan's turn. The two couples' son came and arrived at their homes. The son said, "Ah! This time. We have arrived in your house. Let's see. Are you going to give the mother, the dad or the son [for the tiger to eat]?

Then the son said to the mother and the father, saying, "Ah! Mom and Dad. I see an Orphan... staying down by the big tree. I want to go and bribe him to see if he would come and be my younger brother and we'll [inaudible]." The Orphan's older brother there went and tried to bribe Orphan.

"Younger brother. You come and live with me. If I eat well, you will eat well. If I dress well, you will dress well. I won't let you go and work around the town. If I have food, you will have food. If I have [clothes] to wear, you will have clothes to wear. You go and live with me. You wouldn't have to work at all."

He bribed the Orphan to come and live with him. Orphan went and chopped wood. Orphan went and chopped and chopped and chopped wood. They prepared meat and made rice all ready. Orphan's brother. Orphan's older brother, came and said, "Younger brother, Ger. Go home. We've killed a pig to tie strings on your hands [preparing for a traditional ceremony making the Orphan part of the new family] and to call back your spirits because you've come and lived with me."

[The Orphan speaks:] "Ah! Me! I don't have any so if you are going to call spirits, you eat by yourself. Me, I'm not going to eat. I'm just going to chop woods"

"Go. Go right now. We're going to call your spirits. We're going to cut wood and we're going to call spirits. Then we're going to call

127

spirits. Ah! We already made the meat! Already made the meat and rice ready. Go! We will go and tie our hands as older and younger brother." He kept going at it until Orphan decided to come home [with his newly adopted brother]. Then Orphan came and arrived at home. When he got at home, meat and rice were already packed in the basket. They came home and ate. When they finished eating, he said, "Ah! Hurry up and eat quickly. They told us to send food for the King to eat."

"Then I'll go with you. We'll go and send the food. The King lives down [in] the valley."

"Ah! Then do that. Do that!"

After he finished eating, Orphan and Orphan's older brother. Orphan's older brother was mean so he bribed Orphan. "We are this far. I have sent you this far. There is a huge house just down the valley. You follow this valley and go. You follow this valley and you will reach it. You put down the basket behind you, then get a stick and hit it three times and you stay still inside the house"

Oh! When he reached the house, bones and skulls were scattered all over. He was very scared and frightened. When he arrived here he said, "King. Where is the King? It's just an empty house!" When he arrived there, he left the basket down in front of the house. He took the stick and hit it three times and looked around. Looked around the house and behind it. He saw a huge tall rock. Then he climbed on the rock.

Then the Tiger came and said, "Dog gone fool here! Said he was going to send me lunch. Um. Breakfast for me to eat. How come I don't see it? Where is it?"

"Meat and rice. I've sent there, in the house. Rice. Vegetable… in the house… there. If you are going to eat, then eat. If you are not going to eat, then that's it!"

[The Tiger says to Orphan:] "Get down here!"

[The Orphan says:] "I'm not coming. Dead or alive! I'm going to stay up here. I'm not coming down."

[Tiger:] "If you are not coming down, then I'm coming up."

Then nine eyes and nine noses. He killed and killed and killed *leejxe* [the Tiger] till he was almost done. Then he called his Mom and his Dad. "Hit and you won't hit me. Hit and you won't get me!" The sun was red. It was going to fall. Then he told the Tiger to get down. That tiger… Nine eyes and nine nose. And he will jump down for him to swallow.

This time, the Orphan told the Tiger to close his eyes. So then

Tiger closed his nine eyes and nine nose. Then the Orphan plunged [a knife into] him and he died. But he only carry a small knife. So he cut some stakes and hammered it and finally cut the Tiger's head. Then he carried it and returned. When he got at home, he carried it all morning and arrived home, and said, "Older brother. Older brother. Open the door."

"My dear younger brother, how much money do you want?" [the mean older brother thinks his adopted brother is dead and offers him a bribe in the after life.] "Whatever the amount is, I'll send it later to you."

"Older brother, I have come back for real. I am not lying to you."

"My dear younger brother, Ger. Later, whenever you want money, paper money, don't matter how much, I'll send it to you."

"Older brother. I have come back for real." Then he kicked the door open. He then set the Tiger's head on the side.

[The older brother speaks:] "Huh! You dog!! Why did you go and kill our King dead? This time, they won't be satisfy with you. They won't be happy with you. Why did you go and kill our King dead?"

Then he began lecturing and troubling Orphan so Orphan ran back to the tree. Then Orphan went back and lived by the tree. He went and called. Morning came and he went and called on the townspeople.

"Everyone," he said. "Last night he went and killed the tiger. He killed him himself. He went all by himself and carried it back all by himself. Everyone should go and help him carry the head to go and show it to the King."

Ah! Ten people could not carry it to go and show it to the King. Then the King said, "If that's right, you have killed this Tiger. Well. The Eagle from the heavens have taken my youngest daughter. You must go and get her. If you can get her back, I'll give you my daughter in marriage."

Then the Orphan… Oh! The older brother was mean! So he came back and bribe him. He came and bribe Orphan and again, Orphan went back. Now, this time, he knotted some strings together and tied the King's daughter up and rolled her into a black hole in the Earth. Into that cave, that hole in the Earth. Now Orphan lied and said that Orphan would go and get her. So then he tied Orphan's waist and let him down, slowly down [into] the black hole. Then Orphan reached the bottom and reached the King's youngest daughter. Then the King's daughter asked, "Yes. What are you doing here, child *dab* [Spirit]? You were so scared. Why are you here?"

"Yes. I can come. I have come to help you. Where is the Eagle?" "The Eagle… Later when the sun is about to go down, then the Eagle comes. The Eagle comes and lands on the high branch. The high branch up there. You hide in a good spot. Later, when he comes, you can shoot him."

Ger told Orphan, then Orphan… Oh! Orphan's older brother was already up there waiting. Then Orphan climbed down and asked Ger but they had already hid from Orphan. They hid Orphan. It was dark. The sun was a bit red. The Eagle had return from hunting his prey. The Eagle flew and arrived and landed on the high branch above. Orphan then gave a strong shot at it and the Eagle came tumbling down.

Then Ger said she was too scared. If they could cut bamboo and make baskets, then make two baskets and let Ger go first because she was too scared. And let Orphan go after her. Then Orphan's older brother was mean. Oh! Orphan's older brother was mean so he packed Ger in one basked and said, "All right then, get the silver and gold and break it. One half for Ger and one half for Orphan to make a whole. So later, they can say that's how they got [it].

Then he broke one half to Ger and Orphan one half. He put Ger in the first basket and the other one, he put Orphan in it. Pulled, pulled and pulled. Pushed and pushed. Ger to go. Ger was too afraid so let Ger go first. Pushed Ger til she got up there. Then Orphan's older brother was mean. So he rolled rocks and logs to plug up the black hole in the Earth. It was full. Orphan stayed down there. Orphan didn't have a way out. Then Orphan's older brother took Ger and came home. Then he lied and said, "King. I have freed your daughter."

Orphan stayed and cried and stayed and cried and ran and ran. Orphan's older brother rolled and rolled stones and logs to plug it in. Plugged it up fully. There's no way out! Orphan cried and cried so he sliced up the Eagle to eat and eat and eat till it was done. When he finished eating, the Eagle was very thirsty. He didn't have water to drink. Then the Eagle of the Heavens went and kidnapped the King's youngest son and locked him up, too. He was thirsty for water. King of the Rainbow's son was weeping. Leaking water. He was thirsty for water, so he used the rib of the Eagle to drill and drill and drill til the King of the Rainbow's son came out. Then he said, "Ah! Cousin." He drilled and drilled and said, "Are you human or *dab* [Spirit]?"

[The Orphan answered:] "I am human."

He was leaking water. The rib of the Eagle was used to drill and drill and got him out. Then he [Son of the Rainbow King] said, "Ah! If you are human, then his tools and supplies are under the big rock. You go and get it and carry it back here to open it."

He then went and carried the metal tool to open it. Then King of the Rainbow's son came out. The King of the Rainbow's son said, "You don't cry, Cousin. Now, since you have freed me, I'll pace around three days. I'll pace around for three days till my feet and hands are strong again. I'll take us home. I'll take us home and take you to go and see my Mom and my Dad. You don't rush. You stay still and I'll go and raise a rainbow for my Mom and my Dad to see first."

Then Son of the Rainbow King went to take a shower and raised his colors and stood very high for his Mom and Dad to see. After showering for them to watch, he came back. Came back and made rice and meat. He didn't know. The water was at the end of the cave. He went and carried water to make rice and meat for both of them to eat. After the both of them have eaten, they stayed for three days.

Then Son of the Rainbow King said, "Ah! Cousin. If should you use the bathroom at all, you come and sit on the nape of my neck here like this. And I'll take you. We'll go *daub thiv* [to the other side] up above the clouds. We'll go for three months. But we are going to *daub thiv* [the other side] so we'll just go in three days."

"Ah... If that's right then, Let's make breakfast for us to eat and then we'll go."

Then Orphan finished eating and he said, "Cousin, you come and sit on my neck here and when I bend down, you don't get down. Because if you get down then I will not be able to [inaudible]. You sit still. Whenever I say you can get off, then we can get off. When you have to use the bathroom, you tell me. Okay? And I'll let you down to go and use the bathroom."

[Orphan replies:] "Uh!"

Ah! Then the child rainbow took him and came. They came for three days, three nights. They came and arrived and said, "Ah! Cousin. Since we are here, you get down and I'm going to rise. I'm going to raise rainbow for my Mom and them to watch. I'll call them."

Ah! Then he got down. The son went and called. The mother said, "Pop! My dear son is coming for real!"

The father said, "Mom! Right now our son is some tiger's gold. Some tiger's poop. Ah! Some bear's gold. Some bear's poop."

[But the mother says:] "Pop. Really coming. Coming for real."

Later he called again and said, "Mom and Dad. I'm coming."

[His mother speaks:] "Ney! Pop! My son called and said he is coming for real."

[But the Rainbow King still doesn't believe her.] "Right now our son is some bear's gold. Some bear's poop."

A moment later he [the son] arrived at the door and said, "Mom and Dad. Open the door. I have arrived. I have arrived. Really." Then the mother came out and he said, "Mom and Dad, if you are going to love me then love me but you don't pat on my head. I won't allow you to pat on my head."

Then they cried and hugged and cried and hugged. He went inside the house and bent down, stretched out his neck for Orphan to get down. Bend down his head in front of him. And then Orphan got down and came to sit down. The Mom and Dad were smiling, thinking that in a moment they will have him to eat!

The son said, "Mom and Dad. Don't you do anything bad to make him scared. My cousin here, if it were not for him to come and free me, then I wouldn't be here as your only son. It was very lucky. This cousin has freed me. I am here as your son."

Then the two brothers went out to play. They went out and talked to girlfriends. When they arrived on the road they saw a tiger, a tiger with nine eyes and nine nose like the same one he had seen before. The world, they were divided for him to eat so they couldn't kill him. Then he said, "Ah!" They called for help on their deceased parents but didn't do either. They killed and killed but couldn't kill it. They said, "Ah! If that's right then, you close your nine eyes and nine nose and we'll both just jump in for you to chew." The tiger again. Closed his nine eyes and nine nose. The Orphan then plunged right [into] him and killed him. Again he used that knife to cut the head [off] and carried it to the King to look at.

"Ah! Mom and Dad. And King. This Cousin here. The Tiger. The Eagle. He had killed them. That's how he was able to free me. And now, here, this Tiger here, he killed him, too."

[The King speaks:] "Ah! If you killed this one, too, if that's right then, my dear son, if you want [to] marry, we will give money. If you want any of our daughters, we'll give. Call all over the world, which one you like, and we'll give. You want silver and gold. We'll give it to you."

[The Orphan speaks:] "Ah! We live in the heavens. We cannot have silver and gold. And I can live on *yaj sab* [reality]. I can't live in *yee sab* [your world]. This is all I'm going to say to you. As for me, maybe I'll go back."

Then the cousin said, "Cousin. My dad said, want silver and gold. Don't accept or take them. You just take my Dad's *qeej* [traditional Hmong wind instrument.]

Orphan and the King's Daughter

As told by Mai Yang

A long time ago yes, there was an orphan. Orphan's mom and orphan's dad, they were already dead. Long dead. Then Orphan's mom and dad said, "Orphan, drag us anywhere and see where we will end up. Then the orphan dragged them everywhere and left them wherever they were.

After Orphan's mom and dad died, Orphan dragged his dad and took him down to the banks of the river. Then Orphan said, "Oh!" Orphan was very poor. Orphan asked himself and said, "Oh, what should I do?"

Orphan stayed and watched the river banks. Orphan stayed there until he transformed into a wildcat! Orphan stayed at the river banks and watched after his father. He was very poor.

The King's seven daughters were going to come and choose their husbands. Oh Orphan! Ger's [one of the King's seven daughters] father, the King said, "You go. Whatever you run into, whatever you may buy, buy [have anything] as long as it's a husband. Then you can marry!" The oldest sister started first. When the oldest sister came and arrived at the orphan, Orphan said, "Where are you going, Madam?" "We are on our way to choose husband. On our way to look for husbands."

"Oh! Looking for husband? Then just marry me," [said the Orphan who had been changed into a wild cat.]

"You? A wildcat like you? Who's going to marry you," [the oldest daughter asked]. Then she walk past him.

Then, the second oldest [daughter] came. Then the Orphan asked, "Madam. Where are you heading to?" And she [Ger] said, "We're on our way to look for husbands. On our way to choose son-in-laws."

"Oh! Just marry me," [said the Orphan who was transformed into a wild cat.] "Ha!!! Our dad said that whatever we see, we could have, but I don't want to marry you yet. If I go and can't find anyone, I'll marry you." She went on.

Then, along came the youngest one. It was later when the youngest daughter came. She arrived. Orphan asked, "Madam. Where are you heading to?"

"Me? My dad said that we are on our way to find son-in-laws. But my dad said, "Whomever I met, marry him. Marry them all." "All right then." [said the Orphan]. "If that's right, I'll settle to marry you."

"All right," [said the King's daughter], "then you marry me." Then the Orphan married Ger. Orphan. Orphan was just a wild cat. Orphan had no yard or home to live in. He just lived down by the river banks. Then when Ger got him, Ger took him home. Older Sister #1 and Older Sister #2 were on their way to look for twigs for burning [firewood].

Older Ger and Middle Ger, they went and married Hmongs. They took their two husbands and arrived. Then father-in-law [the King] said, "Older son-in-law and younger son-in-law and middle son-in-law, I want to eat fish. I want to eat fish and I want to eat squirrel, too. Eat doe. Eat deer. *Shai* [antelope]. You guys go and find it for me.

And you guys go and find, I want to eat crabs for me to eat." "Ah! What are we to do so we can find it?" [asked the son-in-law]. "You guys go find in the water. Yes! That's it," [said the father-in-law]. Older Ger and Middle Ger. Their two husbands went all day. They turned every stone over and looked under it. Older Ger's husband got one single crab. Younger Ger's husband got three fish. Middle Ger's [inaudible].Took them home and said, "Ah, Dad, we just couldn't find. We went and searched all day. I only got one crab. That's it. What to do?"

"Ha! Me, Dad. I got three fish. That's about it," [said the second son-in-law]. "Not enough for me to eat," [said the father-in-law]. "All right then. You guys go and hunt squirrels, okay?" They went all day. Didn't get any squirrels. Returned back. "Ah! How come none again?" [asked the father-in-law]. "If that's right, then you go tomorrow. You guys go hunt." [the son-in-laws are thinking.] Oh! Forests are wider than wide. How are we going to go hunt successfully?

Then tomorrow... after eating breakfast, the two brothers [in-law] went all day... And then they said, "Oh, Dad. We went and searched all day... They got nothing. Only one squirrel to bring home." And then they said, "Oh, Dad. We went and searched all day. The forest was very wide. We didn't get to hunt a thing. We didn't see a thing. We didn't succeed in killing anything. Okay."

"Tomorrow," [said the father-in-law], "My wildcat son-in-law. You go and find for me something to eat."

Wildcat son-in-law said, "Dad. They are good with hands and feet. They have hands and feet and they couldn't find. Me? I don't have hands and feet like them. How am I to find?"

"Go," [said the wildcat son-in-law]. "You go look. See if you can find. It must be possible. You go and find."

Then Ger and Orphan went. They went all day. Then the Orphan and them went and spread and spread and spread the net ... and trapped, and trapped, and trapped and got two boats [full of fish] to return. They were gone one whole day till night and returned.

"Dad," [said the wildcat son-in-law]. "I went one whole day. I just only caught two fish and that's it. You wanted to eat. Carry a basket there to go and carry." [Get a basket and go, pick up the fish.]

"Oh my!" Father-in-law got there. [He saw] two boats. All white. [The father-in-law scolds the other sons-in-law.] "You guys... You guys are good with hands and feet. How come you didn't win over my wildcat son-in-law? You guys couldn't go and succeed. Why is it that my wildcat son-in-law here, he got this much and he said he only got two. But he's got a lot?"

[The father-in-law] took it and ate it all. Stayed for quite a while. Then the King [the father-in-law] came and said, "My wildcat son-in-law, you... you go and hunt. See if you can hunt a doe for me to eat. Okay?"

[The wildcat son-in-law speaks.] "What can I do to go and find for you to eat? They have hands and feet. They are good with hands and feet. They couldn't succeed. Me? How am I going to succeed for you to eat?"

[The father-in-law. speaks] "They couldn't go and find, so you go and look for it."

This time, Orphan and Ger, they went and unraveled ropes and unraveled ropes and unraveled ropes under the mountains, under the valleys and filled it up. Then [the doe] was trapped. [They] dragged them all tangled up and bunched together. All came. Dragged ... and arrived on the hills. They were tied to stay up on the hill. [The wildcat son-in-law] returned. Arrived home.

"Ah, Dad. It's night time," [he said]. "Ah ... I just got two ... Let them stay on the top of the hill. If you go, you don't scream. Okay? If you scream, then they escape. You don't scream. Okay? If you scream, then they escape. And you won't have anything to eat."

[The father-in-law speaks] "If that's right, then you take me to go and see them." The Orphan took the father-in-law to go and see. Then the King arrived there. Oh! My! Tied up! All tangled up! Bunched. More than more. Many and more? Oh! Then the wild cat Orphan… The King screamed. And screamed. And screamed. They all escaped except two for the King to eat. That was it.

[The wildcat speaks.] "Father. I told you that you shouldn't scream! Scream! Ha!!! You scream! Scream! Now all have escaped. You haven't any to eat."

Then the King saved two of them. The wildcat got two for the King to eat. The King and the son-in-law went to the farmed fields. Farmed fields! A lot! Three mountains! Three valleys! Then, the King said, "Right now, my son-in-laws, I've found these fields here. And you three son-in-laws here, go and clear the fields till finish."

Then, the two Hmong son-in-laws, they went and clear the fields from place to place. The wildcat son-in-law, he went and just walked on logs. That was all. Then… The two older sisters and the two older brothers gave him a lecture. The son-in-law chide[d] the youngest daughter for marrying the wildcat. "Ger. Ger. Eh! Why marry a husband like you did? Um… Now [why did you] go marry a wildcat like that? He doesn't even know how to work the fields. He just walks on logs and just climbs on logs. Um… Now… Not even working on the field." They lecture. Lecture. Lecture.

Then Ger said, "Dad said, just as long as it was a man, then marry [him]. That's why I just simply marry."

[A son-in-law complains] "Then, Wildcat, that wildcat is a waste of food. That wild cat is just walking on logs. Just climbing on logs. Climbing on logs. Not even working on the field. What to do? Dad left a lot of field for us to do."

They lectured and lectured the wild cat. That night, Wildcat said, "You guys go home completely. Allow me, my single self, to sleep."

Then … that night, they all came home completely. In three days…. three nights, they just completed one mountain. Orphan stayed just one night. Tomorrow, ah! Orphan. Three mountains. Three valleys of fields. All cleared away smoothly, Then. Tomorrow [the brothers] they came. Orphan had finished clearing the fields. All done. Three mountains. Three valleys. All smooth. All done. Then [when the sons-in-law came back they] stay. [They worked together.] Burned the fields. All done. They went and plant rice. Orphan climbed on logs. Walked on logs. Watched them plnt rice. Scattered seeds. Watched pull out weeds then … just watched them plant rice. That was all.

Oh! They lecture, lecture Orphan. They said, "Um. Why is it?

Ger. Ger. She marry a husband. Marry a husband that looks like that? Ah... He doesn't farm. Just walk on logs. Just play and just let [us] work. Ah! Tonight! Go home. [The work] all completed."

Orphan said, "Ger. Ger. You all go completely. I'll just stay. I'll sleep tomorrow. You guys can come [back]. Orphan just slept. They all went home, completely. That night the Orphan planted one night all of their rice. Tomorrow, they came. Then the Orphan had it done. Orphan was just resting.

[One of the daughters speaks:] "Na! You guys were lecturing, lecturing Orphan. You look! Orphan, Ah!!! finished the field, ah! Wild Cat finished the field now. And you guys didn't do it yet. Planting rice all completed. Orphan completing the rice planting. It's time to cultivate the rice. Cultivate rice. Cultivate rice. Ah!

[The lecture begins again.] Wild Cat all day, walked on logs. Wild Cat followed them. [They] cultivating uphill, down-hill, then... Wild Cat was just walking on logs. They were lecturing Wild Cat, "Why is it? Ger. Ger. Wild Cat, Oh! Just walking on logs. Just walking on logs. That's about it. Just simply playing. Not even farming with us." Orphan said, "Ah! Ger. They're lecturing, lecturing me. Tonight, you all go home completely. Let me, my single Self stay." Ger said, "Okay." Then okay.

They went home completely. Orphan then stayed. Then... that night... Orphan cultivated all the rice... completely. Oh! Tomorrow they came... Then ... Orphan had cultivated the field. All done. All smoothly!

[Father speaks.] "Oh! You guys were lecturing, lecturing Wild Cat. See, Wild Cat. My Wild Cat son-in-law doesn't have hands and feet. Ah! How come Wild Cat son-in-law finished the rice fields completely?"

Tomorrow, when they came, farm work was all done. Rice is ripe. Rice is ready then... Orphan... [sons-in-law] all day cut rice stem. Orphan, all day, walked on logs. Play. Climbed on logs, playing... just simply playing. Older Ger, Younger Ger and two older brothers [in-law] lectured. Lectured.

"Ger... Ah! Ger. Why not marry a farm person? [You] marry a wildcat to come and walk on the logs to simply play. How are you going to eat?" Then... Ger and them... They were cutting, cutting rice stems. It was not getting done. Orphan said, "Ger. They're lecturing, lecturing me so you go home with them tonight. You go home with them. Tomorrow you will come. And tomorrow you just send me breakfast for me to eat."

Then... They went... Then tomorrow. Tomorrow they didn't come. Get sent rice, sent rice for Orphan to eat for breakfast. Now Orphan cut [rice stem] one whole night. [He had] finished three mountains. Three valleys. Tomorrow, when Ger came, the rice stems were all cut smoothly. Ger sent breakfast for Orphan to eat. Ger went back [home]. Then Ger sent breakfast for Orphan to eat. All done. Ger went back. Gone... Orphan had gone and made a house. A very fine house out in the open field. Orphan went and made a good house... out in the field. Ger came and told the King.

"Dad. You guys were lecturing, lecturing Wild Cat. Wild Cat finished cutting the rice fields. All clearly done. You guys come. You guys will not see Wild Cat." Orphan already made a house. A house very fine out in the field.

Then Orphan's son... came and told and said, "Ah! King. You guys were lecturing. Lecturing Wild Cat. Wild Cat, ah!!! Wildcat made a house, very good looking, out in the open fields. But you will not see. Do you wish to see? Do you wish to see it? You go with us and you will see. If you go by yourself, then you will not see it. Okay?" King said, "If that's right, then, this morning, I will ride a horse to go see."

Riding the horse. Thumpty. Thump. Thumpty. Thump. On his way to go and see. [The King] arrived there and [there was nothing there.] The King didn't see it anywhere. "Maybe I shall ride chickens!" He rode chickens there. He got there but still didn't see. [He] ride elephants there... But still didn't see either. Then, the son Monkeys came and told the King. "You look here. My armpit and beyond."

Part III

Oral Histories
and Myths

A Journey Home

Sandra Shackelford

You Thoua Lor and his family.
Sandra Shackelford Collection, University of Wisconsin-Green Bay, Archives Department.

Now the three of them—grandfather, You Thoua Lor, grand-mother Chia Moua, and granddaughter Chi Ia Lor—were preparing to leave. They were busily packing up their few belongings for the return flight to Laos and an uncertain future. Grandfather Lor already had their airplane tickets. A council of Lor clan members had come to their house one last time to plead with them, at least for their granddaughter Chi Ia's sake, to stay.

"I'm going back to Laos now," Grandfather Lor said. "I have left some children over there. I have left some here, too. When I am there, I will miss the ones here. When I am here, I will miss the ones there."

Grandfather Lor said, "This heart here, if it could just swallow the wind and the clouds, I would stay hovering between the two countries high up in the sky looking down at the both of them. That way, I would be happy." "But I must go. I must go home now. I wish every one of you well and no sickness."

Across the living room, Chi Ia played "dress-up", wrapping and unwrapping herself, sarong style, in a length of beautiful, bright print fabric. She looked like a young queen, prepared to accept her responsibilities and the future that lay ahead. The three of them would leave Green Bay in the morning. At 5 a.m., a relative would pick them up and drive them to the airport in Milwaukee.

I had brought Chi Ia a parting gift. It was my father's silver watch chain, one he'd been given as a boy by an uncle. The chain was over 100 years old. The links were strong. I attached my crystal pendant to it and showed Chi Ia and her grandparents the moon and the stars that were carved into the silver setting. I told Chi Ia that whenever she lost her way to hold the crystal up to the sun and see in it the faces of all the people who loved her. I clasped the old man's hand, bowed slightly, and thanked him for the precious gift of his stories.

I clasped the old man's hand, bowed slightly, and thanked him for the precious gift of his stories.

Now the People Are Telling it

You Thoua Lor

You Thoua Lor and his family.
Sandra Shackelford Collection, University of Wisconsin-Green Bay, Archives Department.

I am going to tell a story. A myth. A long time ago, elders in historic times called it myth but the stories were events established by people. As time passed many centuries ago, elders called them stories. The people during that time told of certain events. Later these were called stories then they turned into myths because the other people had died and their stories were passed on. That's why they are called myths. Now the people are telling it. Now that the people telling it before have died, it is called a myth. A continuation of Dab and Neej which literally means stories of dead and the living which is called a myth. And now, Yeng Saki.

The Myth of Yeng Saki

You Thoua Lor

Yeng Saki.... He was an orphan. His mom and dad have both passed away. It is called a myth. Back in historic time, people didn't love Orphans' sons. All orphans. Why were they not loved? No luck! They ate vines and leaves from trees. They trapped mice and birds to eat. His parents had passed away leaving nothing. No relatives. No nothing. They would go and work, seasonal farm work, just carrying a small pocket knife. Go and sleep by stumps, behind other's shelter and by the chickens' shack.

As time passed [Yeng] got older. He then could go out and trap mice and birds to eat. He would skin the birds and mice. He then collected the skins and sewed himself clothes out of the skins. Ah...Then he went out to work again and got himself a *qeej* [a Hmong musical instrument] and played it all over the stumps.

Yeng was very poor. As time went on, he learned to play the *Qeej*. He knew how to blow it. Now *Zaj Cace*. Some are *Zaj Nab*. Some are *Zaj Neej*. The ones that are *Zaj Nab*, they are called *Lashe*. They were going to reign again. They gathered themselves together and made arrangements. Then they did this, people came from all over. From under the water and from on land.

It is just like us living in America. When we have a gathering, people from all over come together. From Laos, north and south and across the ocean. Everyone came from everywhere. *Sheng Suelo* is a *Zaj Lo*. He lives in China out in *Tapo*. That's where his older brother lives. He went there back and forth and called everyone to come and eat the feast and drive the carriage. Everyone came to watch. The *qeej* players came. The acrobats came. The musicians came and the beauty queens and the good-looking guys came, too.

Everyone came. They all had parents so they wore nice pants and shirts. Yeng Saki had none so he was in hair cloths. Furs and feathers here and there sticking out of him. When the wind blew, it went right through him. He came and carried his *Qeej*. It was old and it looked bad. It was all broken up.

The parade was ending soon. He watched as everyone played their role. The *qeej* players played their *qeej*. Dancers danced. Everyone played on. Yeng Saki stood there and watched everyone as the chill blew right through his furry clothes. He stood there with the raw smell of mice and birds. "Why.... You brought along your *qeej*? Why are you not playing it?" they asked.

"Oh...! Me? I'm just here to watch. I don't know how to play."

There were many young girls around. In many groups. There were qeej players all in their groups playing. People sang their songs and poets spoke their poems for everyone to listen. You played your-*qeej*. I played my stuff. With all this going on, it convinced Yeng Saki to get involved.

Yeng Saki's *qeej* was bad but all he did in the past was play his *qeej*. When his *qeej* was not sounding, he did all he could to fix it. Yeng Saki played. He played his *qeej*, twisting and turning as he turned the smell of raw mice and bird swooshed from him passed the watchers. He played the *qeej* so loud, it was like the sound of pumpkins rolling downhill.

Yeng Saki played his *qeej*. As he played, many young girls, groups of girls, surrounded him and watched. Everyone was impressed. You were impressed. I was impressed. Everyone was impressed. Oh! Why? Sheng Suelo came and asked, "My... son. You play the *Qeej* so well! What are your parent's names?"

"I don't have any brothers," [said Yeng Saki] "I am the only one left."

[Sheng Suelo] asked and asked Yeng Saki and offered him whiskey and wine to drink but he drank none. "Well, we offered many drinks for you to join us but you didn't drink. Well, how about our daughters here? Do you like them?"

Yeng Saki said, "Oh... I am just an orphan. I have nothing. I don't even have a permanent home. I live among the town. Ah, I just live by stumps. How could I possibly talk to any of your daughters?" "Ah.... [Sheng Suelo said] If you like them, our daughters would like you, too. Come... Come and get to know one another. If our daughters don't like you and you don't like our daughters, well... you can come and just join us. That will please us very much. Oh... Why do you know how to play *qeej* so well?"

Then [Yeng Saki] talked and talked with Sheng Sale, the *Sheng* in town, the *Zale*. He had three daughters and five sons. The *Latoua* was like a president. It's like the Hmong now. The people now. They have the people who are in charge.

Then he said, "My son, if you like us, you are like our brother.

If you like our sisters, our relatives' sisters. These are my sisters. Well, these are sisters from other relatives. These are sisters from the town." Yeng Saki was told about the whereabouts of all the sisters. The youngest sister said, "Latoua. Ask my mom and dad if they allow me to be friend with this brother here."

Latoua said, "Sister Ger. Mother has raised us for this long. We have become man. You have become a woman. Go with your heart. Who ever you like. We are all only human once. Whoever you like, whoever you want to be friends with, go ahead and be friends. If you find you don't like it, let them go. You don't have to ask mother." "Oh! What if I get trouble from mom? Latoua. He then went and asked his parents and they both came out and looked at him. Then the father spoke and said, "My daughters, if you are looking for son-in-laws then marry someone like this. This is what you call a son-in-law."

This gathering was great. It was too great. La She lived in the southern country, way beyond the river *Natale Tale*. They wanted to come and make friends, too. We Hmongs say, "make friends." Others say *la keng* that means friendship, too. Latoua came and held hands. They held tightly. We was very much in love with Latoua's sister, too. He liked her very much. *Zajnab*. He could transform himself into a very handsome guy, too. He could be human. He could be a dragon.

Long ago when life just began, elders say this is how it was. He liked her so much. So he kept his hands by Latoua everywhere. Latoua's sister, She was with Yeng Saki. They blended in with the other young couples.

"Mom and Dad. I am going to go with his *Zajnab* here."

"Dearest daughter. We have just started this year. The year is still very new. Wait till the year is older than you can go. Son, you could go if there is someone else you have interest in. Well, Go ahead and marry him. If there is none that he likes, well, then he can always come back. Let him go. When the time comes, you may go."

"But Daddy. I like him so very much. I'm going to go with him. I have been having fun for two or three days now. I'm not tired of him at all. I am going to go with him."

Then Father went to talk to the brother. Latoua. Latoua is the one who settles all the troubles and situations.

The brother said, "Sister, Ger. Mom and Dad give birth to us. Not too many. Only four of us sons and you guys, only three daughters. If you are going to go and get married, we would at least prepare you a great feast. Let us drink and shed our tears. The year is still very new.

Wait til the year is older. Give him time to set a date. When he comes, we will prepare wine and whiskey for him. We will have a wedding. We will have it traditionally so everyone all over the world can say it was well worth our parents giving birth to us.

Ger started to cry. The time and date of the wedding was given and that was how it was. Cow Month. the 17th … the 18th are only Dragon... the 19th are Tigers Day. Then the 13th month. The 7th month is a Dragon Wedding Day. The 8th month is a Tigers Wedding Day. This is how they kept records of time and days back then. Yes... They made dates and time.

Yeng Saki was going home. But when he was about to leave, Latoua said, "brother, you go. You go and on the Cow Month, the 17th, you return. You come back. We will drink to you. We will give over our sister to you. Everyone will celebrate the wedding. You don't have anything but we do. To say that we don't have anything, well, we do have some. We will prepare it ourselves and have the wedding ourselves. One sister, we are going to give her away through a wedding. Then Yeng Saki left. He left blowing and playing his *qeej,* the sound fading into the distance. He left wearing his ornamental neck piece.

Ger watched as he left. She started to cry. Lashe liked her so much. When he got home, he prepred the wine and whiskey. He prepared everything. Zaj was a very sarcastic person. Zaj went everywhere telling lies to whoever he saw. Lashe was thinking about returning and kidnapping Latouas sister. He was afraid Zaj would find out and lock him up. Lashe tricked Zaj into having drinks with him and then Lashe caught Zaj himself and locked him up. He was locked up in a cave.

Then... Lashe came this time. He came back to take his sister. Latoua said, "Hey...Brother. When I arrived there my mom and my dad...they prepared a meal. They prepared a meal just for me. I am at that age now. They were thinking about someone else to come and persoanlly take you there but was afraid you turn down so I decided to do the honor myself to come here and take you there."

"Then... You come with me and let us go and drink. Go and bless me. Bless me and I will send you back." Yee took him. Latoua thought he was a nice guy so Latoua willingly went along with him.

He came thinking he was there to drink for a good cause but everyone was drinking. They gave him more and more to drink. He got very drunk. He decided to lock Latoua up in the cave. Oh... He was locked up very good. He finally locked him up. Lashe then got him and his people together and was on his way to get Ger.

Everyone was prepared to welcome her. Seng Suelo's youngest daughter. If she was found anywhere, she will be kidnapped. She was seen so she got kidnapped and was taken to the southern world. Yeng Saki was trapping mice and birds. The trapping season was over.

Other people's birds and mice skins were already dry and crisp. They were in several bulk packages. Then... That night Yeng Saki was out trapping birds. He trapped birds all over. Nine hills and ten valleys. He had gone about 20-something days. That night, he walked home and on the way saw an animal, a cat-like animal in the cave. He said, "Brother, where are you coming from?" "I'm just here wandering around for nothing, just looking for birds and looking for mice."

"Oh... Come inside. Come," said the cat-like creature.

"Oh... Brother, if you let me, I would like to borrow your house to rest for awhile. It is going to get dark soon. Can I sleep with you for one night?"

Then... the cat was leading on too much so Yeng Saki ended up spending one night with him. He slept with the cat in his cave. Outside, the cave was a field of farm and a valley. Ahhh...the two of them talked and talked all night. The stars outside were still twinkling. All of a sudden the ground started to shake thunderously. The night was very dark. Trees, rocks, branches and stones rolled down along the hillside. The world was dark outside.

"Oh... Brother. It isn't going to rain is it? I was just outside a moment ago and the stars were still twinkling in the sky. How come it is raining so hard now? Why is the ground shaking so thunderously? It is like an erosion just sliding right past us."

"I can't really say for sure, Brother," said the creature. "The reason is I don't know which one."

"You don't know either?" he asked.

"I don't know."

"Oh, there is something going on, Brother. If it was sunny and the stars were still twinkling a while ago, then it changes to that of rain... it just means you have some work to do." After Yeng was told that, he started to worry.

"Well then, Brother, would you happen to know how to predict any future for me?"

"Future? A little bit. Sometimes the predictions are different. Sometimes they are not."

"Well, if you know how to, then why don't we try? Try and see why all of a sudden a sunny day would change into darkness and why trees and branches and stones are eroding like this and the start, why are they still twinkling like before?"

The cat looked at his knee. He looked at his right knee then at his left knee. He then hit one side of his knee three times. Then he listened. Nothing. He hit his knee again. Again nothing. He hit three times and he listened three times.

The cat then told Yeng Saki, "Brother, from what I have done in the past, there is some kind of work to do. I just worry that somebody is getting married. Getting their wife.

In China. In Tape, China, a girl/boy is on her way. It has been a very long time since I predicted anything. I could be wrong. I don't know. But from what I have done in the past, that is what it is."

"Oh." Yeng Saki was very worried and concerned.

"Well, Brother. Tomorrow when it is clear, I want to go and see. Check to see how far they have gone."

"They both tried to sleep that night but Yeng Saki couldn't sleep at all. Yeng Saki would not sleep whatsoever so he stayed awake and sat around. The cat brother awoke after noticing Yeng Saki could not sleep.

"Brother... You look like you have a lot on your mind."

"Oh... Brother. After listening to what you have to say before, I was thinking I have made a date with Sheng Suelo who lives in China, in Tape, China. I wanted to marry one of his daughters. I was calculating, the month, the time and date has passed. Maybe someone else has her now. I don't know."

They talked and talked til morning. Yeng Saki went to check outside. The valley was filled with rocks and stones. There were stones as big as boxes and ovens. He looked between the valleys of the hills and the sides lined with stones [that] made a clear path through the middle. A shoe with flowers on it was left on one of the stones. He took the shoe and looked at it. Oh! It was Sheng Suelo's shoe [in Tape, China]. Oh... Latouas sister's shoe. It was his sister's shoe. Yeng Saki took the shoe and stuck it in his bag and went on his way. He returned and packed his bag of mice and birds into his basket. He divided the mice and birds with the brother cat and came running back. He slept by a stump. He built a fire and dried the mice and birds. Then he traded them for rice and some food for him to eat. He sharpened his sword and went on his journey. He walked through the path of stones between the valley. He walked for three days and three nights. Soldiers guarded the road. One of them approached Yeng Saki, "Where are you going?"

Yeng Saki could say, "Oh! I am on a mission."

"What kind of mission is it? You have to turn back. If you do not turn back, there is no way to move forward. It is impossible."

"Oh. You want me to turn back? I could do that but if I would run into any kind of trouble, the blame would fall on you. You will have to settle them yourself. What should I do? What am I going to do?"

"Lashe. He is marrying a second wife! He forgot her shoe here. He asked me to follow him carrying this shoe for his wife. That's why I am following right behind him"

"Well, then. Let us have the shoe and we will carry it to her."

"No. I insist." Yeng Saki became very stubborn with them. They argued and argued over who would carry the shoe. The first group of soldiers gave in and let him through. "Let him go," they said. Yeng Saki went on. He went on until he reached the second group of soldiers. Again, he was stubborn. He argued with them. They didn't let him through but Yeng Saki wouldn't go back either. The soldiers were not getting the shoe to bring to their master. They reasoned if the first group let him through, I guess it is okay for us to let him through, too. So they let Yeng Saki go past through them, too.

Yeng Saki went on. He met the third group of soldiers. He knew this was the final group. They had a stone wall built so high behind them. This time nothing got him through. Nine times he had told them to let him through. But none of them let him.

"If you won't let me in, that's fine," said Yeng Saki. "I have already passed two to three groups of soldiers. They let me through. I just won't give you the shoe. If I do, in the future, Latoua, Lashe will not be happy with me. He will not be happy so I will not hand over the shoe to you."

Their conversation continued and they were very convinced. Now the third group of soldiers let him through. This time he found himself standing in front of the entrance. It was in total darkness. When he arrived there, Ger came running out and took Yeng Saki and ran into a hiding place. Lashe came. He was very big. He was bigger than a huge log. His eyes, they were green. Ger took Yeng Saki and ran out the door and ran outside.

Ger said, "Yeng Saki. You... brother... Oh dear brother, if you have followed me, there is a chicken and some rice in this bag here. Take this food and make yourself a meal from it. Eat it and we will talk again."

Then Ger went back inside to Lashe. Now Ger was inside and

Yeng Saki was outside on the other side. The outside of the cave was so wide and spacious and very flat and plain. Yeng Saki was thinking. He then removed a stone and under it was a bag of rice. He lifted it up further and under the stone was a very small pond with three fish in it. He prepared himself a meal from that and slept there overnight.

The next day, just when it was light enough, Ger came out. "Yeng Saki. You have followed me there. My brother has been captured and taken prisoner and punished. They have also captured the news delivery person. Zaj. They called him that, a delivery boy."

"They have imprisoned them both. Why don't you stay here? There are chickens here. You can always butcher them and have them as your food. You stay."

"When the day is a Dragon Day, a dragon will be wet. When the night is a Dragon Night, a dragon will be staying inside. They will want to come out and dry themselves in the sun. Now, in 30 days, they will come out once. They will want to come out and play. If you are going to plan anything, plan it around that time. That is the only way we will ever be able to go have a place to stay, Yeng Saki. This will be the end."

After speaking to Yeng Saki, Ger opened the entrance and went back inside. She didn't have too much time to say much. Many days went by and Yeng Saki lost track of what day it was. He stood around. It was around midnight and Ger cracked open the door and came out to speak to Yeng Saki.

"Yeng Saki," she said, "this is what I'm going to tell you. In just a matter of time, they will come out. The sun will rise and they will come out. They will always come out first. When the sun is out, they are already prepared to sleep in the sun. Whatever you plan to do, it is totally up to you, okay? This way, we could return. If you can't do any-thing, well, you will not be enough for them to destroy you. You are not enough for them to stuff their teeth, Yeng Saki."

Ger then went back inside. She was afraid they might know. Birds started to chirp. The front door slammed shut and out came Lashe. His scales rubbed so hard against the ground as he slid out. Clee' Clee' Clee' Clee'.... He came out. Clee'... Clee'.... Clee'..... He was so long. When he was fully out of the cave, the sky was filled with sunshine. He was so big. He stretched out over the distance of three rice fields. At this time Ger came out.

"Yeng Saki! You have to test him. What are your ideas about getting us out of here? You have to wait when their eyes are gleaming – a gleam so bright, it will light up the forest. When the gleam is everywhere, that's when you are best to plan your scheme. Plan at that time. That's when he is sleeping. When their eyes are green. At that time, don't even dare to move. You don't move. Don't do anything. This is all I'm going to tell you, Yeng Saki."

"Brother. Brother. You watch me and I will watch you. Let's see what you can do."

Then Ger went back in the cave. Suddenly the sun came out. It was high noon. The sun was very straight up in the sky. It was exactly noon. The Dragon's eyes were glowing. The forest was bright... and suddenly, for a while there, his eyes were green again. His eyes were glowing, just teasing Yeng Saki for three times so far. His eyes turned green three times.

His eyes were glowing. Then Yeng Saki... took his sword and did three flips, landing next to Lashe. Yeng Saki raised his sword wanting to cut off the head of the dragon but then he thought... Oh! He was too big! He then did three flips back to the edge of the forest to where he stood before. Yeng Saki was very scared. He was frightened. He had never felt any fear like this before. Yeng Saki's grandpa. He transformed himself into a bird and flew over and landed in front of Yeng Saki.

The bird cried, "Yeng Saki! If you're going to kill him, go ahead and destroy him. If you don't kill him now, in a matter of time, you will not be big enough for them to even stuff their tooth with Yeng Saki"

Then, after listening to the bird cries, Yeng Saki thought to himself, "This time it's live or let die." He did three flips and landed right next to the dragon and gave one powerful strike on his neck, chopping his head right off. Right away the Dragon sprang back to the edge of the forest. Oh! Blood squirted out all over. Streaks of blood ran out as long as an arm, squirting high into the tree tops.

Ger came out and said, "Yeng Saki, dear brother, now this is what I say to you. You stay here, okay? You be real patient and stay here. If we were meant to be one, our fortune would be that we are meant to be a couple. If that is so... no matter what, you and I will be together. I'll go first. You follow behind. We will go together. I will wait for you. We will go together. I will wait for you and we will travel together."

"We will be facing many obstacles. We will be heading for many kinds of problems and situations. Let us go. Let me go first and you stay. If the heavens mean for us to be a couple, there will be a day for us to find each other once again and became a couple. This is all I'm going to say to you, dear"

Yeng Saki cried instantly. "If that's what you say, then I will never get to come back at all."

Sister Ger said that to him. After telling him that, she went into the cave entrance. Everything closed itself up behind her. The entrance was back to a normal big stone. Oh! Yeng Saki had to stay outside. Sister Ger went inside so she came back into the world. She came back to her world, her country, her place. She was back with her parents again.

Yeng Saki stayed behind. He survived by eating the bag of rice that was left behind. When the rice was done, there was nothing else to eat, so he went over to Lashe, the Dragon, and started to cut him up. He cut him up and ate him. He ate Lashe.

There was no water to drink. He walked and walked looking for water to drink. Finally, he saw some water dripping. He picked up a leaf, folded it up to the shape of a cup, and collected the drops. For one night and one day, it filled a whole bamboo shaft. One night and one day, he would get a bamboo shaft. He continued to do this to get his water, but as time went on, the drips stopped and there was no more water coming.

Then Yeng Saki ran out of water to drink. When there was no more water to drink, Yeng Saki took out his sword and knocked on the stone that the water had been coming out of. The stone gave out an empty, hollow sound... Ding! Ding! Ding! A voice came out of the hole. "Are you inhuman or human? Why are you knocking here?"

"Oh... I am human, too." That's how Yeng Saki answered.

"Oh. If you are human, why don't you free me? I am human, too. Let me free and we will go on our way together to our house. Where did you come from?"

"Oh," Yeng Saki said, "Me? I live in the world outside. In China. In Tape. That's where I am from."

Zaj knew this already. Then Zaj said, "Oh, don't tell me. You are my brother-in-law, Yeng Saki, the one that knew how to play the *qeej* so well. You wanted to marry my sister. Are you that person?" Yeng Saki answered. "Yes. I am that person."

The two of them talked and talked. Zaj was joking, bribing him only. He said, "Brother-in-law, what good fortune! Lashe is a mean person. Lashe has locked me up. Now Lashe has kidnapped my sister as a second wife. I beg you to free me. Free me and we will both go back together. I will take you back with me to my sister and do whatever you want. Go and I will give my father's position as King to you. You as King will watch over our country, our Kingdom."

"Oh. I don't know if you are the right person. What if I free you and you are not who you say you are? What if you don't take me back? What do you have to say?"

"Of course, I am going to take you back. You are a brother-in-law. I will always remember you. We were going to have a wedding to accept you but Lashe was a mean person. He bribed me. He wanted to marry my sister. He was afraid I would not permit him to marry her so he locked me up here. If you could free me, we will just go." Yeng Saki decided to free him. "But how will I free you? How will we crush the stone here?"

"Ah, brother-in-law. You just go and prepare yourself a pot of rice. Eat that rice then go and get a hammer and knife from beyond there. Hit just one hard blow and it will break just like that." So Yeng Saki found some rice and made himself a pot of rice to eat. He ate and ate until he was so full but he could not finish it all. Then he went on his way to get the anvil. The anvil was so heavy he couldn't lift it. It was truly heavy. He then went back to the uncle.

"Oh, Uncle. I can't carry the anvil."

"Well, brother-in-law, did you finish all of your rice or not?"

"No. I did not finish it. I was too full. I could not finish it."

"Impossible. You can't do it? You have to finish it. Once you finish all the rice, you will be able to lift and carry the anvil."

Then Yeng Saki went back to finish up the rice. This time he ate all of it. Yeng Saki returned and lifted the anvil. This time the anvil was so light. He carried it over to where Zaj was.

"Oh, Uncle. Where am I to strike it now?"

"Right there," Zaj said. The spot there and here are the thinnest. Move your feet away from the stone so you don't get hit by the fragments."

Then Yeng Saki struck at it. The stone split in half and Zaj came out. Out of the stone flew something that looked like a bat. The stone was empty inside. The space inside was enormous. It probably could fit three or four people but now there was no one inside.

"Uncle," called Yeng Saki.

"Huh?" The word came out from what seemed to be a corner of the stone. Yeng Saki went over to this area where he had heard the voice coming from.

"Uncle, I have freed you. Why don't you come out and talk to me? Why don't you come out and lead the way?"

"Huh? I'm over here." Yeng Saki went to where the voice came from but there was nothing there. Yeng Saki followed the voice for three days and three nights. He called out but all he heard was "Huh. Huh" and "Huh." This continued and it broke Yeng Sakis heart so he finally stopped following the voice.

Yeng Saki left the voice behind. He continued on his way. He followed along. Nothing to eat. He sliced a piece of Lashe then boiled it and ate it. He had plain meat.

He went on his way again. This time he found another water drip. Again he picked up some leaves and laid them down to cover the ground. Next he cut a nice bamboo stalk and set it under the drip. On one day he filled one bamboo shaft. On one night, he filled one bamboo shoot. Everyday Yeng Saki went to the water drop to get his drink of water. As time went on, the water stopped dripping. Yeng Saki then picked up a stone and knocked on the side of the bigger stone.

"Why?" he asks. "This is the spot where water dripped from. How come today there is no water dripping?" He knocked and since Latoua was inside, Latoua heard him.

Latoua asked, "Are you human or inhuman? Why are you knocking here on this stone?"

"Oh. I am human, too," answered Yeng Saki. "How about you?"

"Oh, I am human, too."

"Why are you in there?" Yeng Saki asked.

"Oh, me? I'm just simply angry about my stupidity. I was drinking with these people and I got so drunk. That's how I got in here."

"Who are you?"

"Oh, me? I live in China. In Tape. Ah. He lied to me. He lied. He told me to come and drink and to give him a toast. I came and he just locked me up in here."

"If you are human, too, then, why don't you free me? Who are you?" the voice inside the stone asked.

Yeng Saki said, "Oh, me? I am human, too. I also live in China, in Tape."

"Well, who are you and why are you in this country here?"

"Oh, me! I was celebrating. I was in a parade with all kinds of people. I was celebrating with them. I also had made a date with Latoua and Seng Suelo's youngest daughter. I was going to marry her. But I totally forgot. I went out to trap mice and birds instead. Then...I forgot... Lashe came and kidnapped her so now I am following her here.
Now Latoua knew him. Latoua knew now that this was Yeng Saki.

"Ah, then. Are you Yeng Saki?"

"Yes, I am Yeng Saki. Who are you?"

"I am Latoua. I am Ger's oldest brother. The country and kingdom up there is guarded and protected by me. The reason is because my dad is very old. My father has permitted me to rule it."

The two of them talked and talked and talked. "If you really are Yeng Saki then, let me tell you how to get the chisel and how to drill. It's beyond there. You get it and you come and drill from the water hole. I will knock from inside and we will both crack this stone open. Then we will go. I will go with you and look for my sister. I will go back to my wife and kids and to my parents and bring you to come and live with us, too."

The two of them talked and talked and talked. Then Latoua explained. "Brother-in-law, Yeng Saki. You will not be able to carry it. When you remove one palate, it will have three letters on it. The number one will be on it. Get a stick and lift the stone. Get the rice from under it and make yourself a meal for you to eat."

"There is a stone right by the cave. Lift the stone. Under it will be five fish. There is also water in there, too. Make one full pot of rice. Boil one whole fish. You must eat the full meal and finish all of it. The pot of rice and the whole fish. Once you have done that go and carry the drill from beyond for us to crack open the stone."

Latoua's mom and Latoua's dad plus many of his relatives had paid lightning to strike the stone that was keeping Latoua imprisoned. Lightening struck every day. Striking it made thunderous sounds. It made valleys and hills tremble and shake. It was so loud, it was as if it would just break the stone open, but it only shattered a very small crack. Every day lightening struck. But every day, the stone was as smooth as before. It did not crack open.

Yeng Saki made his rice meal. He ate it and caught a fish. He cooked that, too… and he ate it. He ate and ate. He could not finish it. Oh! Then he went to carry the weapon. The metal shaft was as big as a huge log. It was carved with light sides on it. He tried to move it but it would not even budge.

He went back to the uncle.

"Oh, Uncle," said Yeng Saki. "You have told me to eat the whole meal. I have done that and I could not eat anymore. I tried to carry the metal shaft but I can't even seem to move it a bit. It is too big. How will I ever carry it?"

"Well," asked Uncle, "did you finish your rice? Did you eat all of it?"

"No, I did not finish it, Uncle."

"Eat it all. That's the only way to lift the shaft. The fish. Did you finish the fist, too?"

"No. I did not finish that either," answered Yeng Saki.

"You go back and finish eating it," said Uncle. "And you, when you get the weapon, when you get there... hold onto one end of it and call out saying "Four four corners of the world; Four four corners of the field. Everyone come and help me carry the golden metal shaft to crush the stone."

Lashe's heart is not kind. He has captured my uncle and kept him prisoner for no reason. Please, come and help me carry the arrow and crush the stone and the cave."

"You can lift it now," he told Yeng Saki.

Yeng Saki kept these words in his mind. He came back and sat down and finished all the rice and the fish. Yeng Saki went back to the shaft. The upper part of the arrow was so big! He glanced at the other end and it was as big, too. He looked at the middle section. It was so big! It was as big as a log. There were nine sides to it. It was all green. He tried to move it but he couldn't, not even an inch.

Yeng Saki thought about what Uncle had said. That's what Uncle said. I guess that's what I should say, he thought. Then he held to the weapon with one hand and said, "Four four corners of the world; four four corners of the field. You all come and help me carry the arrow to go and crush the stones and the cave. My uncle has the arrow to go and crush the stones and the cave. My uncle has done no wrong. He has no sins. Lashe was not kind. He wanted to marry his sister. That is why Uncle is kept prisoner here."

Then Yeng Saki lifted the spear. It was so light that he carried it over his shoulder. He went to Latoua. When he reached Latoua he said, "Bother-in-law, you stay a safe distance away. Don't stay too close. Go past the spot where you were staying before. Go way beyond that. Then the shattered rock won't hit you."

Then Yeng Saki went back, past the area where he was staying before and way beyond that, too. He went over three hills and three valleys.

Latoua was inside the cave, the stone. He struck one powerful blow. It was so powerful, the stone blew up. The blow shook the Earth and the stones fell all over the land. They fell in the valleys and in the mountains. Latoua came out. It took Latoua one day and night to get out. Ria was bigger than Lashe.

Yeng Saki was very afraid of Latoua because of his power. And

Yeng Saki was afraid of him… being the way that he was. He didn't know if he was the uncle or not. How come he is a dragon now? And why is he so big? Yeng Saki was indeed afraid of him.

And Latoua was afraid of Yeng Saki. The fact that Yeng Saki was so small. How was it possible for him to kill Lashe? Lashe was so big. How was Yeng Saki able to kill Lashe?

"You are afraid of me. I am afraid of you. Then you don't come near me. I don't come near of you."

Yeng Saki told him that he is truly Yeng Saki but Latoua was still afraid. Yeng Saki was afraid for the fact that Latoua was human before When he was at the celebration and now he was a dragon.

"You tell me to come to you but I won't. I tell you to come to me but you won't," Latoua said. "Yeng Saki, brother-in-law, you must not be small-hearted. Have courage. Stay still. I will take a bath and I will come back." The river was very far away but he was a dragon so he could move very quick.

Yeng Saki stayed where he was. In one blink of an eye, the forest was green for awhile and Latoua was gone. Latoua was gone for a long time. When he came back, he was a very handsome Hmong. He was big and tall and vey handsome.

When he reached Yeng Saki, Yeng Saki told his uncle that he didn't look like him. Yeng Saki said his uncle was a dragon. But his uncle said that it was him. They argued and argued and argued over that. They talked and talked and talked.

"You don't believe me," Uncle said. "I will take you to see my clothes, the clothes I wore when I was taken here. During all this time, they haven't been washed. I left them down there and the fishes there have helped me wash them. There were all kinds of fish that helped me wash them. You don't believe me? I will take you there you get to look at my shirt. My pair of pants. They are still being washed down by the river."

Then Latoua took Yeng Saki down to the river. When they got to the river there was the dragon shell. Each fish had a piece of the shell in its mouth, shaking it in and out of the water, causing waves to rush back and forth from the banks.

"The dragon shell is so big," said Latoua, "Look! Those are my clothes."

This time Yeng Saki believed him. The two of them came back and cooked rice and meat to eat. They stayed together and talked for three days and three nights.

Yeng Saki said, "Uncle... If that's what you say, where are we going to go? Sister Ger has already left and returned to the other side."

"Oh, brother-in-law," said Latoua. "Do not worry. We will look and find our own way back. Together we will leave."

Then Latoua said, "Brother-in-law, let us go and cut some leaves. Let us go and cut us some leaves to wrap some rice in. Then we will go. This way you will have rice for you to eat. We both will have rice to eat."

The two relatives went out to cut leaves to wrap the rice in. They came back and wrapped one whole pot of rice. Then they boiled the rice and made a heap of rice cakes.

"Brother-in-law, you give me this day for me to go and get my clothes to wear. And you, when I am wearing my clothes, you carry these rice cakes right between my chin. You go and sit in there under my chin. If you have to eat, eat in there. If you need to use the bathroom, use in there. If you have to sleep, sleep in there. If we go through the heavens, we will travel for three days. If we go through the fields, we will travel for three months."

If they traveled through the heavens, there was the fear of thunder and wind. So they went by the fields.

"Oh, Uncle," said Yeng Saki, "whichever way you choose to go, we will go. But only one thing. How am I supposed to live in your throat there?"

"Do not be afraid, Brother-in-law," said Uncle. "I have been captured and imprisoned for no sins at all. If it wasn't for you, I would not be free to go back to my country. I will take you to my sister, my mom and my dad."

Now the rice cakes were ready. They were carried and put in Latoua's throat. Yeng Saki was afraid to go and sit in there. Latoua kept telling him to go and sit in there.

Finally, Yeng Saki went inside. Yeng Saki ate rice in his throat. He used the bathroom in there. When Yeng Saki finished carrying all the things, Latoua said, "Enough, Brother-in-law, that's enough. Don't move. Just sit in the same spot and hold on tight. We will go by the [North] fields. It will take us three months. If we go by the heavens, the winds are strong and the thunder so loud. We will be afraid. Therefore we will go by land. Don't make any movement and don't come out."

Latoua made a move. Yeng Saki felt a little movement. Latoua had hopped over one mountain and said, "Brother-in-law, are you still there?"

"Yes, I am still here," answered Yeng Saki.

Latoua jumped again. He jumped over another mountain and valley and he asked, "Brother-in-law, are you still there?"

"Yes. I am still here."

"Brother-in-law, you must not move and surely don't fall out. If you fall out, I will be blamed. It will be my fault."
He asked again and again and again and each time Yeng Saki was still with him.

Yeng Saki and Latoua traveled for three days and three nights. Yeng Saki and Latoua came to rest for one day and one night. Latoua asked, "Are you out of rice yet or not?"

"No," said Yeng Saki. "It is not gone yet."

They continued on. When Latoua jumped, everything shook. But all Yeng Saki felt was just a little shove. They traveled for three months and finally arrived in a city. It was a Laotian city. There was a very big river by the edge of the town.

Latoua and Yeng Saki stopped by the river banks to rest. The rice was finished. Latoua said, "Brother-in-law, Yeng Saki. Why don't you go and beg those *matod* over there for some rice for you? If they have rice ask them to give you rice so we will have enough rice to prepare so we have something for breakfast and lunch to eat. By that time, we will be home."

"Uncle," asked Yeng Saki, "What if I go and they say they won't give us rice? What if the *Matod*, don't give us rice? What are we going to do?"

"Do not be afraid, Brother-in-law. You go. You beg. And if they don't give, just call me and sure enough, they will give you some."
Yeng Saki went. He went and begged and they all said they didn't have any. He begged and begged and they said, "We don't have rice." He went back again and still they said, "We don't have rice."

He begged and begged but he couldn't get any rice. So Yeng Saki called out, "Uncle, I just want you to know I couldn't get any rice."

Then Latoua went down to the river. He made the waves stronger and stronger until they flooded the Laotian city.

Latoua said, "Ask them again, Yeng Saki. This time, see if they will give you any. If not, I will make the water flood up to the village."

Yeng Saki told the Laotians and they said, "Oh, please! Oh, please! However much rice do you want? We will give it to you. Just tell him to stop the water from flooding. Tell him to make the waves smaller. However much rice you want, we will give it to you."

The Laotians went back to get the rice. Yeng Saki said, "Uncle, they are willing to give us rice now."

They gave Yeng Saki one bag of rice. Latoua was laying in the river so the Laotians did not see him. When they went back to the village, Latoua came out of the river as a human form. Then the two relatives, Yeng Saki and Latoua, slept in the Laotians' home. The Laotians saw them as human so they allowed them to sleep in their house that was built up on stilts. That night Yeng Saki and Latoua talked.

Latoua said, "Brother-in-law! There's you. You were able to free me. That's how we got to where we are. That's why I can go back to my family. It is not far to go now. It is not too far away. It is very near. But Latoua was only lying to Yeng Saki. He said that there were only one or two hops and they would be there.

Latoua said "Then... let us go. Let us go tomorrow. If people come. If they come in groups of family and aunts, uncles, villagers. If they pat your head first, then they pat me after you. Now... Brother-in-law, we are going to live in our own country, in our own world."

"Ummm... If I see you, it will be an image. If you see me, it be an image, Brother-in-law. And if they come here and they pat your head first then mine afterwards, we will forever remain as brother-in-law and uncle. We will live together always. When we become rulers or kings, we will live together. We will share the kingdoms and still live together. I wanted to tell you this so you could know, Brother-in-law."

Yeng Saki answered, "Oh, Uncle. If you come and they pat you first, we have to do what I have told you. We will not be able to live together. We will have to live apart from one another. In a different place. In a different country. But if they pat me first, we will live together forever."

The two of them talked and talked and talked and talked. They talked until it was almost morning. They slept for a while and suddenly they woke up and it was light and clear outside. The sun was already out and shining.

They looked outside. The path before them was filled with people. There were so many people. There were people everywhere. But Latoua? He had turned into a rainbow and he had already sent out his message to his parents to come and welcome him home. When they arrived, they patted Yeng Saki's head first. And Ger?

When she arrived, she, too, patted Yeng saying, "Brother-in-law, I have had much luck from heavens above. You came along and freed me. I had thought that you would be my friend and a companion to me and that you were a good person. He lied to me. He took me in as a prisoner, But... Latoua knew the moment he came out of the cave that this was a better place to be. It was the best country there ever is on the Earth. There is everything here. More than 120 things that Latoua could say. It is just the best. Latoua had wanted to return to that country. That is why he planned it like this.

"Brother-in-law. When they arrived here, they first patted your head and then they patted mine. Why don't you go and become my father's king? I am going to go back to where I came from. I am just here to pick up my family. My brothers and my relatives. I am waiting for a brother that has two brothers. I will take that brother with me. I will leave another brother that has two younger brothers to stay with you. We will have the four of us.

"You be my father's king and live in our kingdom, our country. Whenever you miss me during the seventh month when I am unfolding my covers to hang up in the sun, when you look up and see an image beyond the sunset, that is me unfolding my covers to dry in the sun. Whether it is in a spiritual world or in a reality world, that will be the only time you will ever see me [as a rainbow]? As a person living now, remember me always. I will remember you always, Brother-in-law."

They were very sad and very heartbroken. You cried. I cried. Latoua let Yeng Saki be the father-in-law's King. Yeng Saki then became King and owner. He was able to rest forever now in Tapa, China.

Oh, in Tapa, China, Latoua took over Lashe's position. Oh... Za was a comedian. He was a prankster. They had some very tall poles. The 15-foot tall pole was oiled. If Za could climb to the top, he would get a pig thigh. If he failed at it, Za gets nothing. Za was very silly, too. So Za got some sticky sap from the tree branches and rubbed it between his legs. He was able to climb to the top of the pole with no problem, so he got the pig thigh to eat.

Latoua was thinking... "This Za is too tricky. He had tricked my Brother-in-law to follow him through the hills and valleys all over looking for him everywhere. Now that I have sent my brother in-law away to my sister and my parents, he thinks he is bad. I will just tell Pasomehoua to get rid of him."

But Za was a big joker! He was hard to get rid of. No matter how hard they tried, they couldn't kill him. Oh! Latoua looked everywhere to find a person who could kill Za. Then one man said, "Oh... Me... I have nothing to worry about. Me... I could easily trick Za."

"How are you going to trick him?" asked Latoua.

"Me? I will just fart into a bamboo shaft," said the man. "Then I will close it up really good. I will take it to Za and if he smells it, I can surely get rid of him. What do you have to worry about? After that, I will give him some medicine to sniff. Then he will be gone."

"Oh!", Latoua said. "Za's mouth is very tricky. One word spoken by him may mean ten words. He speaks ten words and it is like he speaks 100 words. He means what he says. What he says is what he means. He really means it. Be careful about that. You may not defeat Za."

"Whooooo! Me?" asked the man. "You can even start dividing the land to give me now. I will surely poison him."

Then he went to trick Za. He had farted into a bamboo shaft, sealed it up and went on his way. He went to town and met a man carrying an ax who was on his way to split firewood.

"Where are you going?"

"I'm on my way to split some firewood," the man answered.

"Welcome! Where are you heading?"

"I am just wandering around in your town. Do you know if Za is home at all?"

"Ah! Maybe he is home," said the man with the ax. "When I came here, I saw him by the front door of his house. He should still be home." Then he said, "Well, where are you going? Why are you carrying that shaft? Is it a shaft or salt or a shaft of oil?"

"Ah... I'm just carrying it for fun."

The man with the ax looked at the shaft. It seemed to be empty. Then he asked, "Tell me really. What do you have in there?"

"Ah, Brother," confided the man with the shaft. "Za was very rude. Oh... Latoua told me to bring some medicine to poison him with. But I value my medicine. I do not want to waste it. I thought, let me fart for him to sniff first. If he sniffs the fart first, then I'll use the medicine to kill him afterwards."

"Oh," said the man with the ax. "If you just sealed in a fart, you have come a long way already. You have to open the shaft and sniff it to check and see if it still smells. If it does, then you just close the lid again and go into town. You are sure to meet Za. Then you can take it and let Za sniff it. It's very possible."

"Oh... I guess I do have to smell it first to see if it still stinks."
So the man with the ax opened the end of the shaft and sniffed, "Oh... it still smells all right." Then he shut the lid. Then Za said, "Oh, it still

stinks? Well, if you were the one who farted, and you are the one who sniffed it also, well, of course it still stinks! You would have smelled your own fart!"

"And who is Za?" the man asks?

"Za is me!"

The man was very angry. He was angry that he had not tricked Za into sniffing his own fart.

"Latoua, no wonder you said he was smart and tricky. He told me to smell it to check if it still stunk! I thought he was like every other person in the town. I didn't know it was Za. But after I smelled it, he told me that he was Za. Oh! Za!!! He is evil. Truly.

Latoua thought, "Za is too smart. I might lose this country, the kingdom due to Za's trickiness. I have to go and trick Za myself so that he can marry the King's daughter." Back then in ancient times, the King was like in our generation now. They are our leaders. No one was King. Whoever had the most relatives, they were the toughest, the most powerful. They ruled.

He tricked Za and they tricked the King's daughter, too. It was the King's second daughter, Ger, the second. At first it was just a joke but the King's daughter got in contact with Za. Wherever she went, Za was behind her.

The King was a busy man. The King had work to do. He had a meeting to go to. So he said, "Today your mom went away to buy the flowers." [Flowers were bought then sold to purchase thread and material to make clothing.] "There is no one to watch the house. Ger the second and son-in-law, Za, you two watch the house. I have to go to the meeting," the King said. "When I am done, I will come home."

The house was left for Za and Ger to watch over. They watched the house alright! They played around! You tricked me. I tricked you. They were so busy fooling around with each other that the chickens came inside the house and they didn't even bother to chase them out. The chickens came in and pooped all over the place. Za looked around the house [and] there was just too much chicken poop. He went and got some sugar cubes and sprinkled all over the place to mix with the chicken poop.

It was time for Father-in-law to come home. When he arrived, he said, "Whooo? Why? Ger and son-in-law, you stayed home and didn't even bother to chase out the chickens. Why? There is so much chicken poop!"

"Oh, Dad," said Ger the second. "There's nothing to eat with the

rice. Let the chickens come and poop. We will have it with our rice."
"Are you crazy?" said Father-in-law. "What are you talking about? Eating chicken poop with rice?"

"Really? Chicken poop is very good. Let me collect it." Za picked the sugar cubes into his mouth and ate it and removed the poop into a dust pan.

"That's disgusting, son-in-law. Why are you so disgusting? Why are you eating chicken poop?"

"Why, Dad! Why don't you try it. Really! It's good. It is good with rice, father-in-law."

"Let me taste it then. If it is good, you are just simply a good person. If it's just chicken poop, then you will be killed."

"Alright! I accept, Dad," said Za. Then Za scooped whatever was left of the sugar and let Father-in-law taste it. When he tasted it, father-in-law thought, "Wow! It is really good!"

Then father-in-law said, "Oh! Save it. Save it to be eaten with rice." Father-in-law now has the sugar with rice.

Days later, the father-in-law said, "Son-in-law, today I will let you and Ger stay home again. This time, let the chickens come in and don't chase them out. Later, son-in-law and Ger will scoop up the chicken poop for us to eat with our rice. The other day, the son-in-law had given us some with our rice. It was pretty good. I got full just having it with rice. It is very filling. Now, son-in-law, you two let the chickens come in so we will have some for supper with the rice."

Now Za and Ger let the chickens come in all day. They had forgot to sprinkle the sugar. Later, when father-in-law came home, the son-in-law scooped the chicken poop into the tray. One tray right after another. Tray after tray after tray. They were combined together to make one huge bowl.

"Here, this will be enough to have with the rice," Za said.

"Well... get the rice and set the table and let me taste it," said Father-in-law. Father-in-law tasted it and it was bitter and kind of slippery. It was not sweet like before.

Father-in-law looked at it. He began to get angry. He started to lecture Za. "You! No wonder you were named Za! You match your name very well. You really are tricky."

Latoua said, "Za. He is evil. Let us poison him to death until he dies. Oh! It was Latoua who had spoken of it."

So Father-in-law said, "He lied to me and tricked me into eating chicken poop. Let me poison him to death until he dies."

This time, if Father-in-law poisons him, Za will not escape this at all. Za thought of every solution but they all ended in death. There was no way out. Za was guilty. If he didn't eat, he was guilty. And even if he did eat, he would die.

Za then put a bee in a jug of water. Za spoke to his wife. "Mother. Mother Ger. Ger. If I don't die, it will never end. If I die it will end. I will sit in the chair there. Get my jug of water and set it by my side. When I die, don't cry for me. If, when Father-in-law dies and they are crying over him, then that is when you can cry for me."

After Za spoke to Ger, they prepared to poison the meal and brought it to Za. He ate it. After just two spoons full of juice, his liveliness was gone. He stiffened at the table. His book was set on his lap. A fly buzzed and buzzed around him.

The world was now in silence. There was no sound. No cries. The King now let everyone in to come and see Za. The King came and said, "Ger. Where is your husband?"

"He is reading his book at the table there," she said. "He is still reading... there... at the table there."

The King looked and saw that Za was still sitting there in a lump reading to himself.

Ger turned to the King and said, "Your Highness, he is reading his book. He is sitting there still reading. He already ate. The table has been cleaned already and he is still just sitting there reading his book."

"Whoa!" said the King. The King tasted it and in one spoon, he swallowed it and his live-ness was gone, too.

Oh! Everyone cried for the King. Za's wife saw that everyone was crying so she went to Za and she started to cry, too.

(This is where the myth traditionally ends. What follows is You Thoua Lor's ending.)

At this time now, Za became reincarnated down to this world. But now he had very good ideas.

Those two boys, they call them *I thee loom* in Lao. They were called *I thee loom*. Za stayed that way. He stayed a good person. He was as the person they put in charge to watch over the land, the hills, the mountains and the fields.

The country, *Salab*, this country, in America here, it doesn't have so many mountains, hills and valleys.

I am old now. I didn't have time to go with you to go out and wander with Yeng Saki to see how it looks like. But... when I was in our country, our land... Laos... whenever you called Za... he answered you.

This is what I have to say to all of you: to the sons. To the children. To the daughters. To the sisters. To everyone. In our country, Laos, now that there is no war, there is no Za. Whether it is good or it is bad, we have someone that will watch over it and govern it. Everyone who has a fulfilled life is happier. They know how to live better. If there were no governors, no one to lead like a person who has no parent, it is like this river here. Where there are no stones, there are no fish. Where there is a stone, there is a fish. Where there is leadership and governor, there are people. You think about this. Think about everything.

Being an old person like I am now, I feel that one person is from the old father and one is from the new father. They are the true birth sons. Is the old father or the new father going to love them more? Everyone must think. One person is from the birth mom. One person is from the new mom. Is there more love from the old mom or from the new mom? Everyone must really think about this.

This myth is about being an orphan, about living in this world now. I am talking about the role as an orphan, not just talking about any other kind of people or ants and beetles and bugs. Anyone who is an orphan... no matter who is to say... No one, nobody likes an orphan. But in the end, the heavens help, and they, The orphans, are the ones that get the good standing. The orphans accept many responsibilities. They learn to talk and the elders respect them. Their lives will last them. Whoever was born and their parents pampered them till they were adults. They, in their older years, are very poor. I have never seen anyone like this that is good at all.

This is all I am going to say to you. You have the eyes to look and see for yourself. Love the orphans. Love the one that has no parents, no relatives. Any human called people must know how to love one another. If you know how to miss a person or one person misses another, you must know how to spare a person.

We, as human beings, don't know how to shed our skin. We only die. We have to love one another. This way, it is worth living. My, [You Thoua Lor's] words... this is all I have to say. I wish everyone well. No sickness. Listen to the stories I have told and may everyone live long like the stories here.

[What remains to be translated and transcribed] are stories about leadership, stories about working for other people, stories about spirits, [and] stories about people. There are stories about Adam and Eve. The stars and the trees and the leaves. But they are all very long. It is tiring to tell them. I may not tell them but I have told shorter ones. I have told you a couple of them to listen to.

The reason is because the world is not flat and I am going back to Laos soon. I have left some children over there. I have left some here. When I am there, I will miss the ones here.

This heart here, it could just swallow the wind and the clouds, I would stay hovering between the two countries high up in the sky looking down at both of them. That way I would be happy. I am just saying this for everyone to listen to. I wish everyone of you well and no sickness.

I am just saying this for everyone to listen to.
I wish everyone of you well and no sickness.

Sources

Collum, Maggie. "The 'New Immigrant': One of the Originals in the Shackelford Exhibit." *Voyageur Magazine,* Volume 7, no. 2, Winter/Spring 1991, pp. 2-3

Coonce, Kana. "I Believe in Voice: An Interview with Sandra Shackelford." Available at https://blog.uwgb.edu/teaching-press/2023/11/17/an-interview-with-sandra-shackelford

Erickson, Brenda. "Through Art, One Man's Life Will Forever be Preserved." *Bay Beat.* Np, nd.

Koch, Rita D. "Artist Captures History through Photographs." Friday to Friday section, *Green Bay News-Chronicle*, January 25-February 1, 1991

Meacham, Rebecca, and Olivia Meyer. Personal interviews with Sandra Shackelford, May Lee Lor, Ma Lee Lor, conducted in person and via phone between February 2023 and November 2023.

Shackelford, Sandra. "Artist's Search Leads to Union of Drawings and Documentation." *Voyageur magazine*, Volume 7, no. 2, Winter/Spring 1991, pp. 10-11

Acknowledgements

The author extends special thanks to Joyce Fritz and Don Kraft for their support and assistance, and for being by her side throughout the publication process, along with the Canary Fund, Pete Angilello, and Chris Seidl.

The Teaching Press is grateful for the support, insights, guidance, and time offered by the following people and entities:
- Dr. Pao Lor, Associate Dean of Education, UW-LaCrosse
- Debra Anderson, Archivist, UW-Green Bay Cofrin Libraries, and the Archives staff
- Doua Lor, Southeast Asian Specialist for Safe Harbor of Sheboygan County
- Sara E. Phillips and Diane T. Drexler of the Wisconsin Historical Society Press

The "Southeast Asia" map has been reproduced from *Mai Ya's Long Journey* by Sheila Cohen with permission from the Wisconsin Historical Society Press.

Sandra Shackelford's original 1995 project, "A Portrait of Grief and Courage," which included different and additional stories and photos, was supported by funding from the Hendrickson Foundation.

Other translators and writers associated with versions of this project in since 1991 include Maggie Collum, Mayneng Xiong, and Mee Moua.

About Sandra Shackelford

Sandra Shackelford spent over a decade—from 1956 to 1967—working for civil and human rights in the Mississippi Delta while serving as a member of Pax Christi, a secular institute at St. Francis Information Center in Greenwood. She created a kindergarten based on the teaching methods of Maria Montessori and co-edited what became an early printed voice of the community's Black population. Titled *The Center LIGHT*, the weekly paper sought to fulfill its intention: "give people the light and they will find their way." One morning, the KKK showed its hatred by hurling a firebomb at the newspaper's office, the flames charring the office's white cement block exterior.

Upon return to her birthplace, Green Bay, WI, Sandra worked as a journalist in the Fox Valley, after which she returned to college and finished her BA degree through the University of Wisconsin-Green Bay's returning adults program. Thereafter Sandra taught life-drawing and anatomy at UW-GB and St. Norbert College in De Pere, WI, and co-directed UW-GB's Summer Arts Program for adolescents and teens. She also served as a writing specialist at the College of the

Menominee Nation and was the Integrated Arts Coordinator at Aldo Leopold school, where she used photography and writing as a means for students to integrate classroom learning with the world at large. As a member of the National Storytelling Network, she works with local writers, encouraging them to speak and write their truth.

Sandra furthered her knowledge of the writing process by attending writing conferences and conducting workshops at both the National Story Circle Conference in Austin, TX and The UntitledTown Book and Author Festival in Green Bay.

She is currently at work on her memoir.

Sandra Shackelford at work in her studio in 1991.
Sandra Shackelford Collection, University of Wisconsin-Green Bay, Archives Department.

May Lee Lor, Collaborator and Interpreter

May Lee Lor became a collaborator on this project after working for Northeast Wisconsin Technical College's Family Outreach Program, teaching Hmong refugees how to become adjusted to life in their new country. Lor was born in Laos and moved to Thailand during the Vietnam War, where she and her family lived in a camp for five years before immigrating to the United States in 1980. She moved to Green Bay in 1983. Lor was married in 1984 and now has six children. Throughout her life, she has been extensively involved with the Hmong community, working at the Fort Howard Resource Center, the Hmong Center, and serving as a member of the Green Bay Mayor's Board. She currently works in the Career Center at Preble High School and has since 2011.

Ma Lee Lor, Transcriber and Translator

Ma Lee Lor was born in 1972 in Nasoo, Laos and came to the United States in 1980. As a child, the only life she knew was traveling from village to village, hiding from the Communists. Upon arriving in the United States, her family lived in Virginia for five years on a church sponsorship. She moved to Green Bay in 1985. Lor's first job in Green Bay was working for the Brown County Library, which inspired her passion about education. She also worked for the Fort Howard Resource Center, and she's helped coordinate Hmong pageant shows in Green Bay. Lor has been married for over 35 years and has five children. For the past 25 years, she has worked as a payment specialist at Wisconsin Public Service.

A Note About the Design

Emily Heling, Book Designer

The design of *A Portrait of Grief and Courage* is simple and understated to emphasize the words and stories of Hmong people. As a designer, I wanted to create visual harmony between the storytelling in the book and my use of colors and icons. For the recurring icon at the ends of chapters, I was inspired by stitchwork of the Hmong story cloth. The light purple color seen throughout the book is pulled directly out of a story cloth image included in Sandra's notes for this collection. Through research, I learned that purple is known worldwide as a symbol for spirituality, which echoes the spirituality we learn about in the book, especially in the chapter "The Way of Neeb."

Photographs were also important in the book design. When I first got my hands on the photos from Sandra's collection, I was like a kid in a candy shop. There were hundreds of images to review. When placing the photos into layout, my goal was to evoke the emotions that the speakers conveyed as well as the power of Sandra's artistry when she and I talked about this project.

My biggest design challenge was the cover. I was a brand-new designer at the time I began this project, and the cover is the first task I was asked to tackle. To narrow my ideas, I made PowerPoints of various cover designs and presented these to our staff and Press Director for feedback. As a team, we agreed on the cover design you see before you. We felt the cover photo was a perfect fit, because it's a portrait of a woman who is holding family portrait, and the faces in each photo seem to express both grief and courage. The back cover photo, featuring a beautiful Hmong family and a story cloth, ties together Hmong culture, storytelling, and those left behind in Laos.

Emily Heling is the Book Designer for *A Portrait of Grief and Courage: Hmong Oral Histories and Folktakes*. She was also lead designer for another Press project, *The Viking House Saga*. She will graduate from UW-Green Bay in 2025, with a double major in Design Arts and Spanish Translation, with a minor in Marketing.

www.ingramcontent.com/pod-product-compliance
Lightning Source LLC
Chambersburg PA
CBHW051605120626
46551CB00013B/1678